Women's Gymnastics

KITTY KJELDSEN

Women's Gymnastics Coach,
University of Massachusetts

ALLYN AND BACON, Inc.　　　　　　　　**Boston**

TO MY HUSBAND, ERIK KJELDSEN, WITHOUT WHOSE HELP AND UNDERSTANDING THIS BOOK WOULD NOT HAVE BEEN POSSIBLE.

796.4
K65w

74053
april, 1971

Library of Congress Catalog Card Number: 69–17380

Printed in the United States of America.

Cover photograph courtesy of Russell C. Brown.

Foreword

SPORTS AND OTHER forms of physical activity are an important part of our culture. Recognizing this, Allyn and Bacon has published this distinctive series of books on the basic concepts of a number of physical activities. These books represent a high point in both curriculum design and instructional materials.

The *conceptual approach* has been used in the development of these books. This approach starts with the identification of the *key concepts* around which the activity is structured. These statements, and the sub-concepts which support them, serve as the basis for organizing and relating the facts and skills of the activity into a meaningful whole. The learner is guided in developing these cognitive and motor concepts through a series of *learning experiences*. These experiences are designed to involve him in the learning process, both intellectually and physically. Each experience leads the learner to develop some specific behavior. At the end of each key concept a list of these behaviors (*outcomes*) is given to enable the student to determine if he is learning. If he can demonstrate he has achieved these outcomes, he can be confident that he has conceptualized the material and should be able to perform the activity with some degree of proficiency.

Although these books are designed primarily to be used as supplements to instructional classes, their unique structure and clear presentation can enable a student to learn the activity even without the direction of a teacher if necessary.

The authors have been selected on a national scale. All have excellent backgrounds as performers and teachers in their fields. The combination of these high calibre people and the conceptual organization of the material has produced a series of books which will be of great value in improving instruction in physical education.

Thomas W. Evaul, Temple University
Raymond A. Snyder, University of California

Preface

WOMEN'S GYMNASTICS HAS witnessed a great rebirth in the last 15 years. Suddenly, we are clamoring for more books, more and better prepared teachers, more exhibitions, competitions and clinics. Our young girls have developed a seemingly unsatisfiable appetite for more and more skills in this beautiful sport. Gymnastics itself has become more artistic, creative and daring, qualities very appealing to many youngsters today. All this, plus the resurgence of physical fitness into the national scene, has created a need for teachers with enough background in gymnastics to meet the new challenge.

Many books have been written on the subject during the last five years; most of them are geared to the teacher rather than the student, taking for granted that the teacher has had some background in the sport. The books offer a list of skills at different levels, using the three-pronged approach: "What to do, how to do it, and what are the key points."

On the other hand, more and more books are being written about the "movement education approach" to physical education, where exploration and creativity are emphasized to the utmost, giving very little value to the "formal approach" or direct teaching.

A beginner needs to explore in order to find out what gymnastics is all about. She also needs guidance in this exploration if she is to succeed within a reasonable time and avoid the time-consuming mistakes (often called "bad habits" or "bad shortcuts in skill learning") which others have experienced. She needs to benefit from the experiences of gymnasts before her, without being stifled in the creative aspects of the sport or her own original thought. She also needs the basic understanding of mechanical principles in order to understand what is or is not possible in the field of creative human movement.

Very few teachers are approaching the sport of gymnastics

from this angle. Even fewer books have been written on the subject. An attempt is made here to bridge the gap between stunt teaching (what to do, how to do it and what are the key points) and the movement-exploration-oriented approach. It aims to acquaint the reader with the following areas:

1) Simplified mechanical analysis of the most commonly used movements in gymnastics
2) Guided exploration to basic moves on Olympic apparatus
3) Guided exploration to the field of creative routine construction.

This book is geared to the self-learner, be she a gymnast or a physical educator. There is some evidence that the fundamentals of good gymnastics can be self-taught, provided one fully understands the possibilities and limitations of the human body as a tool to skill exploration. After all, many of the present-day gymnastics coaches are self-taught, having received little or no usable background in the sport during their undergraduate years of professional preparation. Is it not also possible, then, that an interested student can teach herself the fundamentals of the sport if no teacher or coach is available? Or that the teacher and the student can explore the field together, both benefiting from the experience?

The book you are holding right now is a small attempt to cover certain areas of gymnastics in a new way, hoping to shed more light into hitherto dark corners of this fascinating field.

Kitty Kjeldsen

Contents

Concept I—Women's Gymnastics Is a Unique Recreational and Competitive Activity Offering Many Values to the Participant

THE WORD "GYMNASTICS" has several meanings in different parts of the world. The popular Random House dictionary defines it as "the art of gymnastic exercises." In most European countries it means a wide variety of self-testing and creative activities which make up at least one half of their physical education programs. Among many physical educators in America, it has come to mean one specific sport or activity, conducted either with or without apparatus, and having definite basic skills, rules and training methods.

Gymnastics can be recreational or competitive, a team activity or an individual sport. It can be performed using intricate apparatus, or none other than the instrument of the human body. This flexibility gives a wide latitude for creativity and experimentation; however, laws of physics and mechanics often prescribe the most advantageous ways of executing the skills.

1. Women's gymnastics is distinctly different from men's gymnastics.

Unlike many present-day sports, modern gymnastics is not a men's activity modified for girls. This was the case 15 or 20 years ago when women still tried to copy men, performing on flying rings, even parallel bars, side horse exercises and strength-oriented floor work. Modern gymnastics for girls is in many ways a different activity. It takes advantage of the different body build of the female, emphasizes grace, poise and beautiful, flowing movement rather than strength and power.

2. The popularity of this activity in America is increasing rapidly.

Due to these attributes, gymnastics is rapidly gaining in popularity in America. It has always been one of the most popular activities for girls in Europe. The only factor limiting its growth in the United States is a severe shortage of qualified teachers among women physical educators, many of whom acquire little or no background in modern gymnastics during their college years. Wherever introduced under competent leadership, the student reaction has generally been very favorable. The renewed interest in Olympic games and television coverage of the so-called minor sports have introduced the competitive phase of women's gymnastics to large audiences. Our present-day emphasis on fitness has most certainly stimulated interest in the activity.

3. Success in gymnastics is achieved through practice, self-discipline and exploration.

Interest in gymnastics is not limited to one social class or special group. Our main drawbacks for large-scale participation are the above-mentioned lack of qualified instructors and of training facilities with all the necessary equipment. With a proper understanding of the underlying principles and basic concepts, beginning gymnastics skills can be self-taught. This booklet will help you to take the first steps.

To become a good gymnast requires a lot of practice and dedication. On the other hand, it is just as much fun to practice and learn new skills as it is to present them. A practice need never be only a drill of the old elements over and over again. A gymnast in good physical condition seldom becomes "stale," since no one yet has found the limit of skills and modifications of skills in gymnastics that a human body is capable of performing. There are always new fields to explore. Every year brings surprises. Things thought impossible five years ago are performed by many girls today. Things that may seem impossible for us today will be performed by someone tomorrow. This quality can make the pursuit of gymnastics skills very exciting.

On the other hand, only a well-trained instrument is capable of exploring new frontiers. The gymnast's instrument is her body. It should be in as good condition as possible, otherwise the novice will end up with a long line of frustrated attempts. Overweight and muscular softness are the worst enemies of a girl gymnast. Only when every muscle is as strong and every joint as flexible as they possibly can be, only when every extra OUNCE of weight has left the body, can a gymnast explore the exciting possibilities of today and tomorrow in this fast changing sport.

The paragraph above should indicate the personality traits and other qualifications that will produce a successful gymnast. She should have a great deal of self-discipline, courage to try almost anything, willingness to take a certain degree of physical discomfort associated with learning a new skill (sore muscles, black and blue spots) and, above all, an inquiring, creative mind. Body type can also make a difference. Girls of average height, small bone structure and slim hips seem to be more successful than their heavier and taller counterparts, but there are always exceptions to every rule dealing with human beings. The old proverb "where there is a will, there is a way" has a lot of truth in it as far as gymnastics is concerned. Team-sport–oriented students tend to enjoy this sport to a lesser degree than individual-sport girls. Students with ballet, acrobatics or tumbling background are very often one jump ahead of other beginners.

4. There are many values to be gained from participation.

What do you as a student hope to get out of participating in gymnastics?

First, physical fitness and skill in an activity admired by boys and girls alike. Gymnastics is one of the most beautiful sports from the artistic point of view.

Second, you will gain enjoyment from being able to master your body, move well and look good. Flexibility, grace, poise and a good figure can be your rewards. Look at the nationally or internationally known gymnasts—they are the envy of almost every figure-conscious girl.

Third, you will have a chance to explore and create, a chance to represent your club, school or even your country in the competitive field.

Fourth, who knows what might happen? One of our nationally known gymnasts was offered a movie contract several years ago. European and U.S. gymnasts have been beauty queens, representing their country in national or international beauty contests. Gymnastics is a good way to make people notice you.

How much time does it take? The answer to this question depends on your personal objectives. How far do you want to go in gymnastics? All the way? Or is it just an enjoyable recreational activity? Many recreational clubs practice only once or twice a week. On the other hand, our best gymnasts and hopeful Olympic team members spend three to four hours a day, every day, in the gymnasium. Your time allotment depends on your personal goals and the availability of practice facilities.

LEARNING EXPERIENCES

View a women's gymnastics meet and a men's gymnastics meet. What differences do you observe? Do you think the men would be very successful in the women's events, and vice versa? Why, or why not?

Evaluate yourself physically, psychologically, emotionally, intellectually and spiritually. What traits do you have that you feel will help you in gymnastics? What do you think you will have to work hard to overcome?

What do you personally hope to gain from gymnastics? How much time and effort are you willing or able to devote to this? Are your desires and efforts compatible?

Outcomes

After completing this concept, you should be able to:

1. List three different meanings for gymnastics.
2. State three ways women's and men's gymnastics differ.
3. List three reasons gymnastics is gaining in popularity in this country, and cite one factor inhibiting its growth.
4. Explain why gymnastic practice need not be a bore.
5. List five desirable personal qualities of a gymnast.
6. List four potential values inherent in gymnastics.
7. Explain how one's objectives and resources affect each other.

Concept II—The Basic Equipment for a Women's Gymnastics Program Can Be Simple or Complex, Depending on the Level and Purpose of the Program

As STATED IN the previous chapter, gymnastics can be executed with equipment or without, depending on what kind of gymnastic exercises one is pursuing. This book is primarily concerned with the Olympic-style gymnastics and the four international events. These are:

Floor exercise
Balance beam
Uneven parallel bars
Side horse vaulting

Each one of these four events needs different equipment. The dimensions given here are international standards, set up by the International Federation of Gymnastics (FIG). For beginners and young girls, especially in pre-teens, the standards are usually relaxed somewhat. Almost every gymnastics-sponsoring organization has its own set of relaxed standards for youth. So far, we have not been able to agree as a nation on any one set of junior standards.

1. The floor exercise event needs space, but almost no equipment.

It should be performed in an area 12 × 12 meters, or roughly 39'4" square. In most schools and clubs, the bare wood floor is used. Several types of floor exercise mats are available from gymnastics equipment companies, but the cost is relatively high and the mat itself is cumbersome for moving or storing. For a beginner, the floor is perfectly adequate. Regular tumbling mats can be placed at strategic points on the floor during practice at the beginning of the season, to minimize floor bruises. Later, a girl should be able to perform the entire exercise on the floor.

The other item necessary for floor exercise is music. The gymnast will need a record player, tape recorder or pianist, depending on the availability of the latter and the situation in general. Specific records for floor exercise are now obtainable from several companies specializing in educational records.

2. A balance beam can be purchased or homemade.

For beginners either is fine, but more advanced girls should definitely have access to regulation equipment made by a reputable company.

Length of the beam: 5 meters (roughly 16'3")
Width: 10 centimeters (3.9")
Height: 1 meter 20 centimeters (47.2")
Thickness: 16 centimeters (6.3")

The beam should be sturdy, laminated to decrease warping, and should have a nonskid finish. Supports or standards which allow for adjustment in height are a *must* at any skill level.

3. Uneven parallel bars are undergoing many experiments to make them more sturdy and stable, yet bouncy and flexible.

They have presented problems to manufacturers, and are therefore almost impossible to improvise at home. The conversion of men's old parallel bars, once a popular way of economizing, has in most cases proven impractical after a short time. If you are buying any piece of regulation equipment at all, it should definitely be the uneven parallel bars.

Height of the top bar: 2 meters 30 centimeters (7'6.6")
Height of the bottom bar: 1 meter 50 centimeters (4'11.2")

Distance between bars can be adjusted to the length of the girl's torso. The finish of the bars, as in the case of the beam, should be slightly rough and definitely nonskid.

4. The side horse is the same as that used by men, except that girls take the pommels off for vaulting.

Height of the horse: 1 meter 10 centimeters (43.3")

5. The most commonly used beat board (take-off board) is the Reuther board.

It is almost impossible to make at home, but well worth the purchase price.

Height of the board: 12 centimeters (4.7")

The board should have a nonskid wood, rubber or sandpaper-like rough surface.

6. Mats come in many kinds and sizes.

Often the budget of the school or club is the determining factor in the purchase. In general, a good gymnastics mat should be:

a) resilient, without being too thick or heavy
b) easy to carry and store
c) equipped with a nonskid covering or surface
d) available in proper sizes to fit the equipment

Gymnastic chalk, palm guards and tumbling belts (hand-spotting belts) should be added to the inventory as soon as possible. Gymnastic chalk (carbonate of magnesia) is most important for proper care of hands. More advanced girls may also wish to obtain batter's rosin to make the surface of the beam less slippery or to help their shoes give better traction for vaulting.

In selecting equipment, do not overlook the fact that girls enjoy working or exercising in attractive surroundings. All other things being equal, look for equipment design that is pleasing to the eye. Do you know that mats come today in a wide variety of colors? Why should a gymnasium look drab and colorless, when our whole life is so full of color?

Since manufacturers are constantly experimenting with new surfaces and coverings for gymnastic apparatus, the most up-to-date points of maintenance and care can be obtained from them. In general, keep wooden surfaces free of nicks and deep scratches in order to avoid splinters. Periodic sanding might be in order. Store equipment in cool, dry places in order to avoid splitting and warping. Tighten all screws and bolts periodically. Discourage the wearing of jewelry while working on apparatus. Con-

stant rubbing of metal or stone against wood will have its effect
on wooden surfaces. For the same reason, outdoor sneakers or
any other kind of street shoes should never be worn on apparatus.
Gymnastic shoes or socklets are the best; otherwise, advise the
girls to work barefooted. Consult your equipment salesman about
policies concerning replacement for breakage and other problems
that might arise. He can be your best source of help.

7. Personal dress should be comfortable and appropriate to the activity.

Due to the nature of the activity, a leotard is the best thing to
wear for gymnastics. Tights could be worn by a beginner, but
they will soon prove to be too slippery on apparatus and even
unsafe for advanced work. Trunks matching the color of the
leotard will give the girl a secure feeling while she is practicing
and will not interfere with the performance.

It is advisable to remove all jewelry during practices and to
tie back overly long hair. The gymnast should always have an
unobstructed view of the apparatus.

Sneakers do not belong on the apparatus. They are too bulky
for good ankle extension and make the feet look heavy. Work
barefooted or in special slippers available from most equipment
companies.

Concept III—The Basic Movements of Gymnastics Are Governed by the Laws of Physics and Anatomy

AN ARTIST OR musician uses his instrument as the media of creation. He learns to take care of it, and to understand its intricacies and workings to the fullest degree. Often a great pianist refuses to perform on an inferior instrument, considering that as an insult to his ability.

A gymnast uses his or her body to create movement patterns either with or without the help of apparatus. She should learn all she can about the workings of the human body, and be willing to get it and keep it in top-notch condition. Is the condition of your body an insult to your potential? Do you know what kind of performance you can expect from the human body?

The human body is a very complicated machine. The basic laws of physics and mechanics cover its movement. Regardless of all the talk about individual differences, we all have the same basic body build and the same number of joints (there is no such thing, technically, as being "double jointed"), and our actions are governed by the same laws of motion. The important factor is that, with the use of one of the most complicated computers—the human brain—we can make a constant stream of fine changes and subtle adjustments in body position which will give us an almost unlimited field to explore. What is the limit of our possibilities? Has anybody reached it yet?

You are at the beginning of the gymnastic road to exploration. In order to fully understand its possibilities and limitations, it is important to be familiar with the basic concepts of gymnastics. These concepts are based on principles of physics, mechanics and anatomy. Since this is a book for beginners, only the most basic ones are discussed here. For further information, consult books in mechanical analysis of movement, kinesiology or physics.

1. The wider the base of support and the lower the center of gravity, the more stable the body.

In an upright position, we are supported by our feet. We have, since early childhood, learned to make constant adjustments in our muscular tension in order to be balanced in this position. Watching a small child learn to stand and walk will bring back to us the long forgotten fact that balancing on one's feet is a skill which has to be mastered by trial and error at an early age. Since it was learned when we were very young, we are no longer conscious of trying to balance ourselves on our feet—it happens automatically most of the time.

The body can also be balanced and supported on the head and hands (headstand), on the hands only (handstand), on the buttocks (V sit) or in several other ways. Since these positions are not natural to our daily living, we must at first consciously fight for balance. In order to obtain the best possible results in the least possible time, it is necessary for us to understand the laws of physics governing stability and balance. Beginning skills of gymnastics deal mostly with these two conditions of stability:

a) The lower the center of gravity, the more stable the body.
b) The wider the base of support, the more stable the body.

What is the *center of gravity?* According to N. H. Black in *An Introductory Course in College Physics,* the center of gravity of a body is the point at which we can consider its whole weight to be centered. A regularly shaped body will balance if supported at its center of gravity. Any change in the shape of the body or in distribution of its mass will change the location of the center of gravity. In some irregularly shaped objects the center of gravity can be outside of the body.

In the human body, standing in the upright position, the center of gravity is generally in the hip region, varying slightly with the body type of the person. In males, the center of gravity is generally higher than in females. The location of the center of gravity is not constant, but changes with any change in body position. As mentioned above, it can be inside or outside the

Figure 1. Examples of the Approximate Location of the Center of Gravity in Different Positions

body. In situations where there is no movement, as long as the center of gravity is OVER the base of support, we are in balance. If it falls outside, we have to fight for balance. When movement forces are introduced, this may or may not be true. Balance is, then, the result of the dynamic forces involved.

LEARNING EXPERIENCE—STABILITY AND BALANCE
Stand up straight, feet hip-width apart, arms down to the sides. Reduce your base of support by standing with both legs together. Which feels more stable? Raise your center of gravity by lifting both arms over your head and further reduce the base of support by raising up on your toes. What happens? Diminish your base of support even more by standing only on one foot, with your arms still overhead. What happens to your balance? Why?

A very common gymnastics position is the *inverted support* or *handstand*. As in regular standing, good body alignment is necessary in order to reduce strain on muscles and to keep the center of gravity over the base of support. The base of support is smaller (hands instead of feet) and, with girls, the center of gravity is higher in this position. Big-hipped females are especially un-stable, having a much harder time in balancing than their slim-hipped sisters. Another common mistake is sagging at the waist: this puts too much strain on the lower back, is uncomfortable as a position and is esthetically unbecoming.

LEARNING EXPERIENCE—INVERTED SUPPORT

Walk up to a wall. Stand tall, raise your arms overhead and mark the height that your fingertips can reach without standing on tiptoes. Now put your hands on the floor and kick your feet up against the wall. If you have never done it before, put a mat next to the wall and have a "spotter" guide your feet to the right spot. Keep your elbows straight, look down at your fingertips, pull in your abdomen and stretch your body as tall as possible. Do your toes touch the mark?

Feel this body position in order to try to simulate it later. Push away from the wall gently with your toes and try to balance. Do not let your body "sag." Touch the mark with your toes every now and then for reference.

Do not expect to balance on your hands as easily as you do on your feet. A good handstand with proper body alignment takes a lot of practice. A gymnastic handstand should have only a gentle arch from head to toes, NOT a sharp bend or C curve in the lower back region.

2. The hanging support and swing is dependent upon a firm palmar grip and a tight shoulder girdle.

For this, you will need something high to hang from. It can be an overhead ladder, a horizontal bar or just a sturdy piece of wood or metal. The best would be the high bar of uneven paral-lel bars.

LEARNING EXPERIENCE—THE GRIP

Hang from the bar, grasping it with your fingers facing forward. Place your thumbs around the bar. Next time place your thumb along your index finger and take a higher grip, so that your palms are in contact with the bar. (This is called the palmar *grip.) Which feels more secure? Which way can you hang longer?*

LEARNING EXPERIENCE–HANGING POSITION
Hang with the palmar grip and relax at the shoulders, letting yourself sag. After awhile you will feel uncomfortable. Try to draw your knees up without tightening at your shoulders. What happens?

Hang again, using the palmar grip, but right from the beginning lift up the shoulders so your ears come up closer to your elbows. Keeping your shoulder girdle tight, try to pull your knees up to the chest. What happens?

From these experiments, you will find that it does make a difference how you hang. The palmar grip is stronger than the finger grip. Keeping tight at your shoulders enables you to control your body during the hang and makes it possible to execute skills you would find difficult to do while sagging at the shoulder girdle. *Try to remember the feel of a controlled hang, and utilize it whenever hanging is called for.*

2a. Your body moves as a single unit in the pendulum swing, with a moment of weightlessness at the end of each swing. In gymnastics we use two kinds of swinging movements: the *pendulum swing* and the *beat swing*. Each one has a

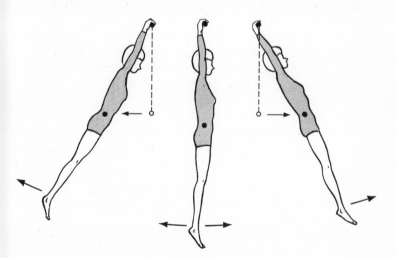

Figure 2.   The Pendulum Swing

different purpose. In a pendulum swing, your body moves as one unit. You are the string of the pendulum, with the weight at the point of center of gravity. The *point of rotation* (a fixed point around which you rotate) is the bar in your hands.

LEARNING EXPERIENCE—PENDULUM SWING
Jump to hang from the bar and have a friend gently push you at the center of gravity, just as one would push a child on the swing. As you are swinging, feel the timing of the pendular action. Notice the momentary stop before change in direction at the end of each swing. Many stunts are executed at that momentary weightless phase at the end of the pendular path. Feel the acceleration *or "downbeat" after weightlessness, and the slowing-down phase after you pass the vertical (straight up and down) position. Some stunts are executed during the* deceleration *phase of the swing. Be able to feel and anticipate different parts of the swinging movement.*

2b. Alternately piking and arching your body while hanging will generate a beat swing. In the *pendulum* swing, your body is a single unit pivoting around a stationary object—the bar. In the *beat* swing, there is an attempt to use the natural flexibility of the bar to assist the gymnast. The center of gravity remains under the bar at all times. By alternately arching and piking your body, an attempt is made to depress the bar. When sufficient force has been created and the bar sufficiently depressed, the upward lift of the bar is utilized to add lifting force to your body. While the gymnast's body is thus moving upward, desired changes in position can be made with relative ease.

LEARNING EXPERIENCE—UTILIZATION OF THE
BEAT SWING
Hang from the top bar of the uneven parallel bars, or any other convenient bar (if the bar lacks flexibility, the desired effect and feeling will not be there). Try to lift up your legs, keeping your knees straight. How high can you get them? On your next attempt begin by arching, then piking, again arching and piking your body (as in Fig. 3) and see how high you can lift your legs on the second forward swing. Which was easier and more efficient? Which method enables you to attain more height?

Try to feel the "beating" action of the bar and work with it. Make sure you drop your weight on the bar at the vertical position between each forward and backward swing.

Figure 3.   Positions and Location of Center of Gravity in the Beat Swing

3. Rotation, in mechanical terms, means movement of a body around a fixed point called the axis.

According to Geoffrey Dyson in "The Mechanics of Athletics," the axis of a revolving body is a straight line, itself at rest in the body, about which all the other parts rotate or spin." For an easier description of movement, here are the main axes in the human body (see Fig. 4).

Imagine these axes as being pins or rods through the human body, piercing the center of gravity. In each rotational movement we revolve around one of them. For example:

Transverse axis—Forward roll
Longitudinal axis—Pirouette or full turn
Medial axis—Cartwheel

The axis can be real (rotation of your body around a bar), or imaginary (forward roll). It can be stationary (rotation around a bar), or can move with the body (forward roll).

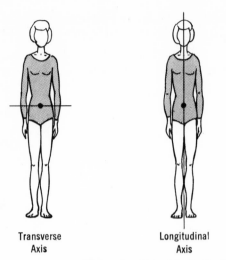

| Transverse | Longitudinal | Medial |
| Axis | Axis | Axis |

Figure 4.   Main Axes in the Human Body

3a. The speed of the body rotating around a fixed point is determined by the length of the radius of rotation.

LEARNING EXPERIENCE—ROTATION

Execute a forward roll in a tightly tucked position, with your knees and chin as close to your chest as possible. Now do one in a loose, half-tucked position, then one in the piked position. Which was the fastest? Which one took less force to execute?

Perform a pirouette or full turn on one foot, with the other held out behind you. Hold your arms out to the sides. Do it again, but half way through the turn pull in your arms and leg. Now start the turn with your arms crossed over your chest and your free leg held next to your body. Half way through the turn, stretch out. What happens?

From this experiment, one can conclude that the smaller or tighter your body the faster it rotates. Spreading out your arms in the pirouette or loosening the tuck in the forward roll will slow down your rotation. In technical terms: *with a given force, the shorter the radius of rotation the faster the speed of rotation.* Lengthening the radius of rotation will slow down the movement; shortening will speed it up. This idea of slowing or speeding up rotation during a movement is used in executing many stunts, especially on the uneven parallel bars.

4. The body can assume three basic positions in each phase of movement.

Almost every teacher or coach who has written about gymnastics has his or her own list of basic body positions as part of his movement vocabulary. Many times the lists are quite long, being different for each piece of apparatus. An attempt is made here to consolidate many of these positions, and to come up with a short list of basic ones which apply to all gymnastic events. First, we will examine the *phases* of movement in which the basic positions are used.

4a. The body moves in support, hang and flight.

a) *Support:* The idea of support has been discussed already. A body can be supported in many different ways, and will remain in balance as long as the center of gravity remains over the base of support.

b) *Hang:* Hanging has also been discussed. Besides the regular long hang, there are combinations of supports and hangs, or hangs from a different part of the body (knee hang).

c) *Flight:* This phase includes everything done during the short time that a gymnast is free from external supports, such as during the flight phase of a vault, on the trampoline or in aerial tumbling. The laws of *gravity, action-reaction* and *ballistic flight* govern what happens during this brief moment of relative weightlessness. Most of their applications will be apparent during intermediate and advanced gymnastics.

During each of these phases of movement, the body can assume three basic positions: *tuck, pike* or *layout.* Many people use these terms in their everyday vocabulary, but have you ever had them defined? Usually we see these positions and associate the proper terms with them. Can you explain them verbally? In technical terms, *we can decrease or increase the angle of every joint.* From this point of view, we will examine the three basic body positions.

a) *Tuck:* The tuck position consists of decreasing the angles of the hip and knee joints. The smaller the angles, the tighter the tuck. For better body position, the chin is usually brought to the chest, hands clasping the shins, unless the arms are otherwise used.

b) *Pike:* The pike position consists of decreasing the angle of the hip joints only. For better body position, the back should be straight, with the knee and ankle joints extended.

c) *Layout:* The layout refers to total body extension, usually with a very slight total body arch. The term *extension* refers to increasing the angle of a joint. When 180 degrees is exceeded, it is usually referred to as *hyperextension.*

Tuck   Pike   Layout

Figure 5. Three Basic Body Positions

5. Upper body flexibility is very important in girls' gymnastics.

It refers to the hyperextension of the upper back and shoulder joints, and is used mostly in backbend-related movements such as walkovers or limbers (see Fig. 17). Care should be taken not to confuse it with the lower back arch, which means hyperextension of the lower back region. Since the lower back seems able to take much less strain than the upper back, the substituting of one type of flexibility for another in backbend-related movements can lead to lower back problems. Shoulder stretching can be

Wrong   Wrong   Right

Figure 6.   Upper Body Flexibility

somewhat uncomfortable, and takes time to develop, but there are no short cuts which can safely be taken.

6. The front and back split is a simultaneous flexion at one hip joint and a hyperextension of the other.

The torso in the basic split position should be vertical, not leaning forward or twisting to the side. Only when you have mastered the basic split should you experiment with different body positions and arm movements. The back knee in the basic split should be turned under, facing the floor. A slight turnout is often more pleasant to look at and, to many girls, easier to execute, but it restricts movements through the split position. Much depends on the girl's hip flexibility. In general, held split positions are more attractive with a slight turnout. For movements through the split position, a more basic split should be used.

The *side split* means a 90-degree abduction of both hip joints. It is much harder to execute and not as easy to blend with other gymnastic movements, especially at the beginner's level.

7. Head position and sensory cues are important factors in women's gymnastics.

In most beginning gymnastic moves, the head is held erect and in line with the body. The use of a head movement when it is not called for (*e.g.,* thrusting the head back while executing a backward hip circle on uneven parallel bars) can throw the entire body out of the correct position and make the stunt much harder, if not impossible to complete. On the other hand, some stunts depend on a definite and prescribed head movement for completion. In these cases, the head position should be explained, either by the coach or in the book describing the move. A common fault by the beginner is the overuse of the head. Remember—*keep it steady unless instructed otherwise.*

8. Visual and kinesthetic cues are important for the spatial orientation of the gymnast.

A beginner often does not know where she is during the execution of a move, and therefore finds it difficult to correct any mistakes. Giving her something to look at (her legs, the bar) during certain parts of the move will greatly improve that lost, empty feeling and help to bring forth kinesthetic awareness of her body position.

Outcomes

After studying this concept, you should be able to:
1. Explain why all human bodies generally react the same.
2. List four different bases of support on which the body can be balanced.
3. Explain the relationship between the base of support and center of gravity and balance.
4. Explain why inverted balance is more difficult than standing balance.
5. Demonstrate the correct grip and shoulder position in a hanging position.
6. Name and demonstrate the two types of swings, and explain the differences between the two.
7. Define rotation, and state the rule that governs the speed of rotation.
8. Identify and name the three axes of rotation of the human body, and demonstrate one movement of rotation around each.
9. Name and define the three phases of movement.
10. List and demonstrate the three basic body positions.

11. Describe the difference between upper and lower back arch.
12. State which type of back arch is best for gymnastics, and explain why this is so.
13. List the two types of splits, and demonstrate one of them if you can.
14. Explain why head position is important in executing gymnastic movements.
15. Explain the role of visual and kinesthetic cues in gymnastics.

Concept IV—The Four Olympic Events Are Floor Exercise, Balance Beam, Vaulting and Uneven Parallel Bars

IT IS HARD to cover in one chapter four areas about each of which an entire book could be written. Therefore, it becomes necessary to be selective. The emphasis in this book will be on the first steps necessary for the beginner, and on routine construction.

1. A floor exercise routine should consist of dance, acrobatics and tumbling movements in artistic succession, with interesting choreography, change of pace, mood and the level of performance.

For a beginner, this seems like a huge task. She may very well ask: But where do I start?

Start with the basic locomotor movements and move to composition as soon as possible, even if you do not have all the skills you would like to have for your floor exercise routine. Too many girls learn the so-called floor exercise stunts first, and then find they do not know how to put them together. A lesson can be taken from the teachers of modern dance—start practicing choreography early, even with only a few basic skills. The most important thing is lots of imagination.

1a. A variety of rolls are used in floor exercise.
Step-out forward roll: Assume a squat position. Reach forward with both hands, put them down and lean forward until part of your body weight is supported by the hands. Tuck your head between the arms and bring your hips over your head by pushing off the mat with both legs. Place the back of the neck on the mat and start rolling over. During the roll flex one knee, keeping the other extended. At the end of the roll reach forward with both hands, step first on one foot and then the other. For a

Figure 7.   Step-Out Forward Roll

more difficult stunt stand up on one foot only, holding the other up in front.

Backward shoulder roll: From a sitting position on the floor, start rolling backward with the right knee bent and the left one straight. As you get on your back, lean your head to the left and keep the right arm straight out to the side. Put your left palm on the floor over your left shoulder, fingers facing your shoulder, elbow pointing up. Continue rolling, placing your right knee to the mat over the right shoulder. Your left leg stays off the ground. Roll over the right shoulder and push off with the arms to a knee scale position. The entire stunt can, of course, be reversed.

Upper back roll: Kneel on your right knee, with your left leg straight out to the side, touching the mat. Your arms are held out to the sides. Round your back and place your right shoulder down on the mat in front and to the left of your right knee. Your right arm should reach under the left leg. Transfer your weight to the right shoulder, roll over your upper back and up to the bent left knee, with the right leg stretched out to the side on the mat. Your upper body should be straight up, with arms out to the sides.

Figure 8.   Backward Shoulder Roll

Double-knee shoulder roll: Start a backward roll. When you get on your back, place both arms out to the sides, lean your head to the left and bring both knees over the right shoulder. Transfer the body weight to the knees without using your arms. Come up to a kneeling position.

To learn the following two rolls, you will probably need a spotter. Working in groups of three is very good for beginners, and can keep everybody busy in large group situations. One girl is executing the stunt and two are spotting, one on either side.

Handstand: This stunt can be attempted fairly early in the gymnastics career, providing you have a good understanding of the upside-down position (see Concept III, Inverted support) and can handle your body weight in a straight arm support.

Stand with one foot in front of the other (the foot you usually kick with should be in the back). Bending the knee of the front leg, reach down with both arms. The elbows should be kept straight. Place your palms on the floor, with fingers facing forward and hands about shoulder width apart. At the same time, kick up with the back leg and push with the front leg until the knee is straight. As soon as you feel the hips overhead, bring both legs together and straighten the body in an upside-down position. Pull in your abdomen and focus your eyes on the mat slightly above the fingertips. Point your toes and reach for the ceiling with the entire body, trying to straighten it as much as possible.

The timing of the kick is important here. Boys usually place their hands on the floor before kicking up. This style is harder and less attractive for girls. Kick up as soon as your palms touch the floor.

A handstand could be practiced against the wall or with spotters. In order to be most helpful, the spotters should stand to the sides of the performer and catch her thighs with both hands when she reaches the upside-down position. The grip is best around the knee joint: grab around the knee with both hands and steady the performer. In case only one spotter is present, she should take hold of the leg that kicks up first.

Handstand forward roll: Kick to a good handstand (no arch, body straight) between the two spotters. The spotters should face each other and take hold of your legs just below the knees, in order to keep you in balance. Make sure your center of gravity is over the base of support, your arms are straight and your head is slightly up. Look at your fingertips. Bend your elbows, looking

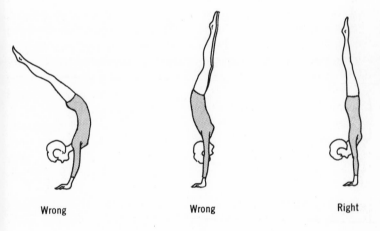

Wrong   Wrong   Right

Figure 9.   Handstand

at the mat, until there is just enough room left to get the head through. Tuck your head, placing the weight gently on the back of the neck, round your back, pull the knees down to the chest and execute a forward roll. The spotters should lower your legs until you are safely on your back, then release. Step out of the roll.

Backward extension roll: Execute a slow backward roll and stop halfway through, with the weight supported by the back of your neck and arms. Keep your hips up off the floor, and knees pulled to the chest. Spotters on either side will now grasp your leg below the knee on their side. On the count of THREE (given by you), they will pull you up and you will extend at the same time, until you reach a handstand position. Now try the entire stunt without stopping. Execute a backward roll between your spotters. (They will have to step in quickly to get in position.) When you feel that your weight is over the shoulders and arms, extend with the help of the spotters. Later, try it alone.

How many combinations of the rolls listed here can you come up with? Over what other part of the body can you roll? Can you change the direction of the roll halfway through? Remember

Balance   Lower   Tuck   Roll

Figure 10.   Handstand Forward Roll

—*the smaller your radius of rotation, the faster you will rotate.* Can you execute these rolls at different speeds? Change the speed halfway through?

1b. A turn is a rotation along the vertical axis (same as the longitudinal axis in the upright position). It can be executed on one foot (*pirouette* type) or on two feet (*pivot* type); it can be ½, ¾, one or more revolutions, or anything in between. The body position can be in tuck, pike or layout, as long as the center of gravity is over the base of support. Out-of-balance turns can be very exciting, but they require a very delicate condition of off-balance to keep from stumbling or falling. They are, however, well worth experimenting with. Arms can be literally in any position, depending on the effect desired. In certain turns, your arms can help in initiating or stopping rotary motion. They can also be helpful in changing speed during a turn.

Pivot turn: Stand with one foot in front of the other, with your feet close together. Rise up on the balls of your feet and turn around. End up facing the opposite direction, with the other foot in front.

Pirouette turn: Step on the ball of your front foot. Swing the rear leg, with bent knee, across in front of the supporting foot and turn around the vertical axis.

Cross-over turn: Step sideways on your right foot, cross the left over the right and execute a pivot turn to the right.

Kick turn: Step on your left foot, with the right one held up off the floor behind you. Swing the right foot forward and kick it up in front. At the height of the kick, turn to the left on the ball of the left foot. Finish facing the opposite direction, with your right foot up in back.

LEARNING EXPERIENCE—TURNS AND VARIATIONS
How can you modify these turns? What possibilities are there for the arms? What positions can the free leg take in turns executed on one foot? Can these turns be executed in squat or pike positions?

Turns in the air: Almost all the above-mentioned turns can be executed with a jump during the turning phase of the move. What other ways can you execute a turn in the air?

Tour Jeté: Execute a kick turn in the air, but change your feet before landing and land on the other foot. This turn is usually done with a gliding step-together-step preparation (chassé or glissade).

LEARNING EXPERIENCE—TURNS AND VARIATIONS
What other parts of your body can you turn on? Seat, knee, hip, arms, upper back? How can you get these turns started? What about arm and leg positions? How many of the turns described above can you execute on body parts other than legs?

1c. Leaps and jumps are means of getting off the ground and moving in a linear direction as well. They should be executed in a light, airy and soundless manner, giving the illusion of a momentary stop at the top of a leap. Watch good ballet dancers: they are a perfect example.

What is the difference between a leap and a jump?

Leaps: I) take off on one foot and land on the other
Jumps: 1) take off from both feet and land on both feet
       2) take off from one and land on both
       3) take off from both and land on one

Body positions during flight are:

A) Tuck
B) Pike
C) Layout, with following variations:
    a) straight legs
    b) split legs
    c) stag legs (split with one knee bent)
    d) straddle legs
    e) big arch
    f) ankles crossed

LEARNING EXPERIENCE—LEAPS AND JUMPS
Try to put these combinations together. How many leaps and jumps can you come up with? What kind of arm positions can you add to these combinations? For example, 1Cb is a split jump, 1Bd a straddle

jump. What would 1A look like? 3Cf? 1Ce? This listing can be carried further. You can add another column for arm positions, one for head positions, etc. It should be a good beginning for a girl who does not know where to start.

Remember—*all leaps and jumps should be taken off from a semi-squat position.* The thrust off the floor is very fast, with an extension of the leg in all joints, finishing up with the maximum push from the toes. The direction should be up as well as forward, or backward, diagonal or sideways, depending on the direction one wishes to travel during that particular stunt. After leaving the floor, the body will assume the necessary position for that particular leap or jump. Hold your breath at the top of the height, but make sure that the shoulders are down, not up around your ears, regardless of the position of the arms. Break out of the body position just before landing and come down into a semi-bent knee position; contact the floor with the toes first, then the heel, then bend at the knees and hips. Exhale during landing.

LEARNING EXPERIENCE—FLOOR EXERCISE COMPOSITION
Take three 5 × 7 or similar size tumbling mats and put them on the floor about 10–15 feet apart, as in Fig. 11. If mats are not available, mark the floor with rectangles. Put on some music to get yourself into the proper mood (many girls will feel very self-conscious at first, so music will help them to relax and divert their attention from themselves to what they are supposed to be doing), and start by following the assignments of composition:

1. *Execute a roll on the first mat (any kind of roll), leap or jump over the second and do a different roll on the third mat. Go back to the beginning and repeat the sequence with different components.*

2. *Leap over the first mat, execute a turn on the floor between the mats, roll on the second mat, do a turn in the air between the mats, jump on the last mat, and do a turn on a body part other than your feet on the floor after leaving the mat.*

3. *Leap in front of the first mat. Land and immediately execute a roll on the mat. Execute fast consecutive turns between the mats into a different kind of roll on the second mat. Jump, land on the third mat and immediately go into a roll. Finish with a low half-turn on the floor and go back between the mats with a series of leaps.*

4. *Use your own imagination to continue from there.*

The same method can be used when experimenting with floor exercise composition in larger groups. Place mats in a similar formation, making three or four rows rather than one. Have girls lined up, four or five in front of each mat. Decide on an assignment and put on music. The first girls should start when the music starts. The second ones should follow them as soon as the first girls are halfway down the row of mats, and so on. The girls should come back between the rows of mats and start all over again with a different combination.

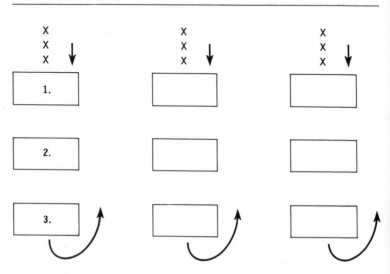

Figure 11.   Mat Formations for Floor Exercise Composition

1d. Poses are used to spice up a floor exercise routine and to provide for change of pace. Only one or two poses should be held during the exercise, and they should be of the kind that you can do really well. Others should be used only for transition, either to finish a sequence of moves, to change direction or to emphasize a particular note or chord in the music. The classic pose in gymnastics is the *scale* (a variation of *arabesque*), but variations of it, as well as other positions of momentary balance, are almost limitless. One note of caution—*if you are not flexible enough to execute a good scale, do not attempt it.* There is nothing more unpleasant looking than a "sick" scale held during a routine.

Since the number of poses and their variations can be almost limitless, a beginner may obtain many ideas from the following chart. Once again, this list could be expanded to include other body parts or more listings under the same headings, but the attempt here is to start out in a more simplified manner.

Support on	Arms	Legs
1—two feet	A—straight	I—straight
2—one foot	B—curved	II—bent
3—buttocks	C—one curved,	III—one straight,
4—hand(s) and knee(s)	other straight	other bent
5—hands only	D—elbows bent	
6—knee(s) only		o—in front
7—knee and foot	a—up over head	oo—to the side
	b—diagonally up	ooo—in back
	c—in front of the	
Head	body	x—in close to the
	d—diagonally	body
/—in line with body	down	xx—out hori-
//—looking up	e—diagonally	zontal
///—looking down	back	xxx—below hori-
////—turned to the side	f—out to the	zontal
	sides	xxxx—above hori-
	g—front and back	zontal
	h—diagonally	
	front and back	
	i—one over head,	
	other out to	
	the side	

LEARNING EXPERIENCE—FLOOR EXERCISE COMPOSITION
Choose four easy-to-remember poses (1–2–3–4), some up, some down. Move slowly from one to another (1–2–3–4), then back up again (4–3–2–1). Take four counts for each change, or use music in the background and take two to four measures to move from one pose to the next. Repeat the sequence with four new and more intricate poses. Combine your next sequence with some locomotor assignments from the previous learning experience. An entire beginner's floor exercise routine can be built around these basic patterns.

Figure 12.   Variations of the Scale Position

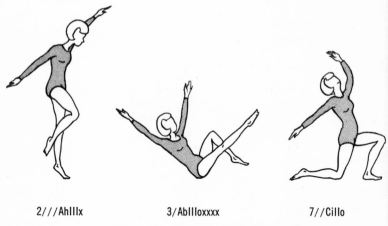

2///Ahlllx   3/Ablllloxxxx   7//Cillo

Figure 13.   Examples of the Poses

Here are some other ideas for creating floor exercise patterns:

1. Hitch kick (scissors kick), cartwheel, twist out to face the direction of travel, step into a scale, then forward roll to 3/AbIIIoxxxx pose.
2. Cartwheel, tour jeté landing in the scale position, swing the back leg forward, sit down and immediately execute a double

knee backward shoulder roll, ending up in 6//Ab position, sitting on heels.

3. V-sit to backward shoulder roll, stand up, kick turn, swing back leg forward and handstand forward roll.

4. 2///BgIIIx pose. Arms curved down. Open out the bent leg in the back and execute a ¼ turn toward it. Glissade, tour jeté, twist out in the direction of movement and cartwheel to scale. Kick to handstand, forward roll, come up on both feet and execute 1Ca jump with arms overhead, with a slight arch in the upper back during the flight. Upon landing, bounce right into 3Ca jump, opening legs up in the air and landing with one foot up in back.

No right or left directions are given here. Try these combinations on your favorite side. If needed, a beginner could take a step between the moves in the combinations in order to end up on the preferred foot. More advanced girls, however, should be able to execute these simple skills to either side. Modify these combinations or continue them, adding your own ideas. If you cannot execute a handstand forward roll alone, place a mat at the proper place and have a spotter assist you.

Without going into more difficult elements, you can now make up a short floor exercise routine. Take a piece of paper and map out a simple floor pattern; for example:

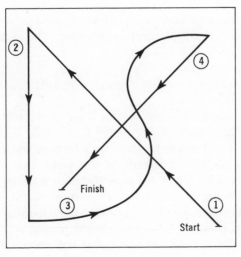

Figure 14.   Floor Pattern

Keep it simple and short at first. Now try to visualize combinations fitting this pattern. The first pass is straight and fairly long, crossing the area on a diagonal. Get a good opening sequence of locomotor movements, leaps and jumps for a lively beginning. The next pass carries you along the side. It can contain slower movements, preferably big ones that cover distance. Now you come to the S curve. Such moves as rolls and turns could be used for constant change of direction. Move from pose to pose, mixing in rolls, turns, steps and acrobatic moves. The entire S curve should be executed smoothly. The finish is another diagonal pass for lively locomotor movements.

This is one interpretation of the floor pattern. You could come up with another, completely different one.

Draw another floor pattern. It does not have to follow the fast-slow-fast pattern. If you have found music that you like, try to draw up a floor pattern while listening to it. Harmonize your pattern to the musical phrases (for example, end a pass when the melody or rhythm comes to a logical stop). Later, when you become more experienced, try to work against the basic beat. Syncopate it. Let your imagination run wild. Use elements from modern jazz, currently popular dance styles, ethnic dances and other movement ideas. Change pace and direction where it is least expected, but keep the change logical. Have an unusual or surprise ending.

Are you ready for new moves? It will depend on your strength, flexibility and overall physical conditioning. The examples given here should not be too difficult.

1e. Handstand combinations require balance, strength and good body control.

Cartwheel: Stand with one foot in front of the other, as if attempting a handstand. Your kicking foot should be back. Bend the front leg and reach forward with both hands. So far, it is very similar to the handstand. At this point, twist your upper body so that if the right leg is in the lead, your right shoulder is turned toward the right leg. Place your hands on the mat directly under your shoulders, one at a time, kicking sideways to a handstand position. Your legs should remain separated. Pass through the handstand and bring your legs down one at a time (see Fig. 15). After you become more experienced, you can experiment with a true side cartwheel, starting and ending up sideways. It is important to keep up good body alignment, as in all inverted supports. Your arms should be straight, with no arch in your lower back or piking action at the hips. Your head should stay up, eyes focusing on the floor slightly in front of the fingertips. Your body weight should pass over one hand at a time, then over the first foot that contacts, and then over the second one.

Figure 15.   Cartwheel

Tuck lower: Cartwheel or kick to a handstand position. At the top of the handstand, bend your knees and pull them slowly toward the chest. Lower to a squat or kneeling position. While trying to get the feel of the move, have a spotter steady your hips, pulling them gently over your head during the lowering phase, then letting them down (remember—*your center of gravity has to stay over the base of support*).

Straddle lower: Cartwheel to a handstand and straddle the legs. Pike slowly, bringing the straddled legs down (hips move over the head). If you are strong and flexible enough, hold the heels off the floor until your buttocks touch and then execute a backward roll. A partner can help to balance your hips.

Figure 16.   Straddle Lower

1f. Backbend movements make use of the arch in the upper back. Can you push up off the floor into a good backbend? Lower down into one from a standing position? If yes, you might be ready for the following series:

Handstand arch over (front limber): Kick to a handstand between two spotters. The spotters will steady the backs of your thighs with one hand, while reaching down with the other to take hold of your upper arm (thumbs out grip). Start to lower your legs, arching from the UPPER BACK. The spotters will let you lower your legs to the floor, pulling gently at the same time at your upper arm in order to help you up. Remember—*head stays back, chest arched.* Thrust your hips forward upon landing. The spotters will help you get the feel of the move without fear of falling. Later, try it alone.

Front walkover: Kick to a split handstand (legs in the split position) between two spotters. They join one hand across and let your hips rest on it, while reaching down with the other hand to take hold of your upper arm. Arch over and land on one foot at a time. Remember—*for any archover or walkover moves, the arch in the upper back is very important.* For a controlled and slow lowering of the legs, the center of gravity should stay as close

Start   Right   Wrong

Figure 17.   Front Walkover

to the base of support as possible. As your legs start to lower, push your chest out over your arms in order to increase the arch in the upper back. Otherwise, your legs will fall down uncontrolled.

Back walkover: Go down slowly into a backbend from a stride standing position (one foot in front of the other). As your hands touch the floor and before the body weight is transferred onto them, kick up with the lead leg. Go through a split handstand to a standing position. Spotters should kneel on either side and put one hand under the middle of your back in order to slow down the backbend phase on the move. The other hand goes behind the buttocks and assists in pushing them over the head. Again, the arch should be in the upper back, and the chest should be moved forward over the hands as soon as the hands touch the ground.

Yogi handstand: Kick into a handstand. Pike at the hips, lowering the legs, and lift the head up; look for your knees. In order to keep balance in this position, the hips should be far over the head. This requires very loose shoulders. Stretch back up to a split handstand and walk out of it. The head movement is very important here. During the handstand, look down at the

(a)   (b)   (c)

Figure 18.   Yogi Handstand

fingers. As the hips move over the head and the legs lower, the head comes forward and the gymnast looks for the knees. During the straightening phase, the head returns to its original position and stays back during the walkover.

> *1g. A large number of movements can be terminated in a split.* Can you execute a good split yet? If so, try to experiment with the following combinations:

Forward roll to split
Backward roll to split
Cartwheel to split
Kick turn to split
Handstand lowers to split (tuck and straddle)
Walkovers to split
Yogi handstand to split (drop to split from position b, Fig. 18)

Many girls find it much harder to get out of splits than to get into them. Here are some hints for getting out of split positions, letting you finish the combination:

1. From a split, twist into a straddle sit and . . .
2. Lean toward the front leg, swing the back one around to front and . . .

3. Pull up and back into a kneeling position on the back knee and . . .
4. Put your hands down to your sides. Lift the hips, pulling legs together into pike position and . . .

When most of the previous moves are mastered, you are ready for more advanced skills.

There are many good tumbling and acrobatics books on the market, describing a wide variety of skills. As you master new skills, try to incorporate them into your floor exercise routine.

2. Work on the balance beam is moving closer and closer to floor exercise executed on a four-inch surface.

Many of the basic skills are the same, but a lot harder to execute, requiring more precision, balance and just plain nerve. Unfortunately, too many girls learn stunts on the beam before having mastered the basic locomotor movements. As a result, their work lacks sureness and fluidity which could make even simple beam routines a pleasure to watch. There is nothing more boring or ugly for an audience to watch than a slow, wobbly and unsure though technically difficult beam routine.

It is a good idea to practice all beam skills on the floor first. A gymnasium floor usually has an ample number of painted lines which can be used as imaginary balance beams. Later, you can use a low but regulation-width balance beam, and then a high one.

LEARNING EXPERIENCE—WALKING ON THE BEAM
Hold your body erect, head up. Keep your arms out to the sides, shoulders down, neck long and graceful. Start walking up and down the beam. Point your toes, stepping on the ball of the foot first. Focus your eyes on the end of the beam, and later on the floor straight ahead of you. Speed up the walk until you are almost running, staying on the balls of the feet and elongating the steps. In order to practice running without slowing down, climb up at one end, run across and jump off the other end.

An entire class can be kept active practicing this way. Have the girls climb up on the beam at one end and run across, one after the other, the second girl starting as soon as the first girl has taken three steps. To make the climbing easier and less time-consuming, place a chair in front of one end of the beam and have the girls step on it on their way up. As soon as a girl jumps off, she should go back into line. Encourage the line to move fast, until the girls are running on the beam. Almost all locomotor movements can be practiced this way.

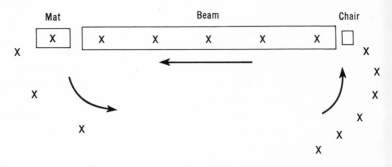

Figure 19.   Group Organization on the Balance Beam

2a. Many dance steps can be executed on the balance beam. Try these combinations, using at least two or three beam lengths for each:

1. Step-together-step, step-together-step.
2. Step-together-step-hop.
3. Step-hop, step-hop.
4. Step-kick (forward with a straight leg), step-kick.
5. Grapevine step sidewise (crossover step).

Think back to different folk and social dances. Are there any other steps you could adapt to the balance beam?

2b. In general, jumps are easier to execute on the beam than leaps, since the focus of the eyes will generally remain in the same place—in front of you on the beam. All jumps should be taken off from a semi-squat position and landed the same way. For beginners, the eyes should focus low on the beam. More advanced girls can attempt to look away from the beam at the height of the jump; this makes the jumps harder to execute, but also much more exciting to watch.

Simple jump: Stand on the beam, one foot in front of the other. Jump up and land in the same foot position. Point your toes and pull the legs close together in the air.

Jump, single change: Start the same way as above, but change feet in the air and land with the other foot in front.

Tuck jump: Stand with one foot in front of the other. Jump, pulling the knees up in the air. Straighten out before landing.

Jump, half turn: Stand with one foot in front of the other. Jump, execute a half turn and land facing the other way. For a beginner, it is easier at first to turn in the direction of the back foot.

Here are some more difficult variations:

Jump with a double or triple change in the air.

Tuck jump with a half or full turn in the air.

Jump with a total body arch in the air, arms over head. Break out of it before landing.

Split jump—assume a split position at the top of the jump, pull the legs together prior to landing.

Refer back to the floor exercise section for additional jumps.

2c. Since leaps cover ground (although there are some exceptions), the focus should stay low but move along the beam. Beginners should not attempt to look away, although this is done by advanced gymnasts.

Hitch kick: Kick up your feet in front, one at a time. Switch in the air and land on the foot that left the beam first.

Cat leap: Do this the same way as the hitch kick, but execute it with bent knees. Make sure that your toes are pointed all the way through. Many girls tend to flex their ankles when knees are bent.

Long leap: Take off from one foot and land on the other, covering as much ground as possible.

Split leap: Do this the same way as above, but try for height as well as distance and assume a split position in the air.

Refer to the floor exercise section for other possible leaps and their variations.

Your shoulders should stay stationary during the take-off for leaps and jumps. Do not let them raise up around your ears. The push should come from the legs, not from an obvious lift of the shoulders and arms.

2d. Turns on the balance beam are very similar to floor exercise. Remember, while practicing turns—*have a point of focus at the beginning and at the end of your turn; this helps you to keep erect and to retain your balance.* Turn around the longitudinal axis, and avoid leaning in any direction. Execute the turn on the balls of your feet. Step into turns on one foot, moving your weight forward over the ball of the foot, which will be your base of support.

LEARNING EXPERIENCE—TURNS ON THE BEAM
Can you execute the following turns on the beam?

pivot turn
pirouette turn
cross-over turn
kick turn
tour jeté

They are explained more fully in the floor exercise section. Try turning on the seat with your feet up, on one knee and in other positions. Can you turn in the half-squat-half-straddle position?

Here are some more difficult variations of the turns:

full turn on one foot
full knee turn (hands are on the beam to push off, body is almost horizontal, other leg is up in back)
full turn in the air

2e. Up to three poses can be held in a competitive beam routine in order to show control and provide for change of pace. This is a good guideline to follow even in noncompetitive or beginners' routines. Other poses, as in floor exercise, should be used only for transition. Refer back to the floor exercise chart for an unlimited supply of fresh ideas. The classic pose is again the scale, but be careful to use it only if it looks good the way you do it. Remember—on the beam, you are on a pedestal. The viewer sees you at a different angle, so every flaw is much more apparent. Some commonly used poses on the beam are:

Knee Scale   Lunge   Toe Touch in Squat Position

Figure 20.   Poses

Without going into rolls, supports or acrobatic moves, you should have enough material to compose several beginners' routines. Here, as in floor exercise, it is beneficial to start exercising your creative talents early. Mark out the length of the beam on the floor. Forgetting for a moment the need for a mount and dismount, start making up series of locomotor movements, jumps, leaps and poses that will carry you from one end of the beam to the other. Keep your combinations simple and flowing. There should be no unnecessary steps or shifts of weight between the component parts. On the floor they will be less obvious, but on the balance beam every little fault can be noticed. Arm movements are very important. Keep them moving through different positions, and try to avoid keeping your arms merely out to the sides for any length of time. Move backward and sideways as well as forward. Use some poses sideways or diagonal to the beam. If, as a beginner, you have to look at the beam during the steps, leaps and turns, make sure to look off and assume different head positions during the poses. Many girls enjoy practicing beam routines to music; this might help you in changing the rhythm and quality of your movements.

LEARNING EXPERIENCE—ROUTINE CONSTRUCTION ON THE BEAM

Take a piece of paper or an index card and write down your routine, pass by pass. Try it on the floor, then on the beam, having someone read the moves out to you until the routine is memorized. Critique each other for form and execution. If something does not look good, change it.

After having mastered the basic locomotor movements, turns and poses on the beam, you will be ready for more challenging elements of beam work. Each of the following stunts should be understood first, then practiced on the floor, on the low beam and finally on the high beam. Use spotters (working in groups of threes can again be a good idea) until the moves become familiar enough to be executed alone.

A few words about spotting beam work in general are needed here. During the basic locomotor movements, turns and poses, spotting is not too essential. A beginner can have a partner walking along side, holding her hand at first, but this practice should be discontinued as soon as the girl feels confident enough to move up and down the beam unassisted. The best way to spot a beginner after that phase is to stand an arm's length away, holding up your hand. Do not touch her, but let her take hold of your hand if she feels it necessary. Make sure there is enough room for her to jump off and clear the beam if she loses her balance beyond control. She should not have to be afraid of landing on you. Above all, avoid any impulse to grab her legs when you see her fighting for balance. Let her take hold of you or jump off, whichever she prefers.

On the other hand, skills requiring inverted support or a feet-over-head position should be spotted at first. The spotter should either support, guide, push or pull at the performer's center of gravity (around the hip region, in most cases), making sure it stays over or moves along the beam. As the performer becomes more skillful, ease up on spotting; it should be a girl's dream to execute the move entirely on her own.

2f. Rolls are basically the same as in floor exercise, but have to be executed with more precision and slowly at first. Hand positions are important.

Backward shoulder roll: By now, you should know from floor exercise how to execute one on the floor and over which shoulder you will be rolling (let's say it is the right shoulder). Jump on the beam and lie down on your back. The spotters should help to stabilize you at the center of gravity. Put your head down along the left side of the beam, bring your arms over your head and hold onto the beam from underneath, with your elbows close together. Bend the knees and start lifting legs over head. (Later, it should be executed with straight legs.) Place the right knee on the beam over the right shoulder (as close as possible), transfer your weight over the knee, place hands on top of the beam and come to a knee scale position.

During the roll phase, the spotters should place their hands on either side of the performer's hips and guide them straight over head.

Forward head roll: The starting position is the squat position on the beam. Place your hands about 18–24 inches in front of your feet, definitely in front of your shoulders, thumbs on top of the beam, fingers down to the sides of the beam. Bend the elbows and raise the hips over head. Tuck the head and place the back of your neck on the beam, between your hands and feet. (Do not roll forward over the top of the head.) Stay in a tight pike. Now change your grip from top of the beam to the bottom, keeping your elbows close to your ears, and roll forward until your back is on the beam, with your feet pointing toward the ceiling. Lift your hands and head off the beam and continue rolling to a straddle sitting position. The spotter should stand at the side of the beam, facing the performer's hips. She should place one hand on either side of the performer's hips, and steady them while her head is being tucked, then guide her hips down the beam.

For variations—start a forward roll from a lunge or scale position. Execute one from a straight legged stand. For a more advanced roll, do not change your hands from top to bottom or pause momentarily on your back. Keep the hands on top and roll right over, ending back up on your feet.

LEARNING EXPERIENCE—ROLLS ON THE BEAM
How many other ways can you get up from a forward roll on the beam? Is it possible to execute a dive forward roll? Can you do a forward roll without using your hands?

Backward head roll: Start from a supine position. Place your hands behind your head on the beam, with the thumbs about one or two inches from the top of your head and your fingers down to the sides of the beam. Pull your knees up to the chest and roll until the hips are over the shoulders and part of the weight is on the hands. Extend the hips, pushing with the hands at the same time to clear the head. Land on the beam with one or two feet (in a squat position at first), and transfer your weight over them.

The backward head roll is somewhat unique in its timing. The roll is not executed in one smooth movement, but gains additional momentum from the extension of the hips. It is not slow and controlled like the backward shoulder roll, but more similar to a backward extension roll in tumbling.

The spotter helps to lift the hips during extension (one hand on either side of your hips) and guides them straight over head.

For variations—execute backward rolls without extension. This requires a very flexible neck. Start like a regular roll, but keep rolling smoothly over the head and land in a squat position or on the shins on the beam. The legs should be placed as close to the head as possible. Transfer the weight over the legs and push with the arms to clear your head.

Balance   Roll   Extend   Transfer Weight

Figure 21.   Backward Head Roll

2g. *Inverted supports open up a completely new field in beam work.* They require a lot of practice and the ability to control a handstand on the floor. Only the most basic ones are discussed here.

Cartwheel to side handstand: Practice on a line on the floor. Place your hands down one at a time, kick up, stop in the handstand position and bring your legs together. Keep your elbows straight, your head up and your body stretched toward the ceiling. Try it on the low beam, with a spotter steadying the hips at the handstand position (she stands behind you).

Before attempting the move on the high beam, practice coming down from it during under or overbalance. If you are underbalanced, just snap down, ending up facing the beam. In case of overbalance, execute a ¼ twist to the right or left and snap down to the far side of the beam, ending up sideways to it.

Spotters will not be able to reach your hips when you are on the high beam. Steadying the upper arms during the handstand position will be sufficient.

For variations—after you can hold or control a side handstand on the beam, try a handstand squat lower and a handstand straddle lower (these skills are explained in the floor exercise section).

English   Side   Split English

Figure 22.   Handstands on the Beam

English handstand: Since the correct hand position is impossible to execute on the floor, start on the low beam between two spotters. The spotters can stand on benches or chairs if they are not up high enough.

Stand on the beam with one foot in front of the other. Place your hands down on the beam (thumbs together on top, fingers down to the sides) and kick up to a handstand. Keeping your arms straight, look up at the beam; stretch your toes toward the ceiling.

Spotters can steady the performer by taking hold of her legs just below the knees (each spotter holds the leg closest to her) until she is ready to come down. Then they can lower her down gently.

Split combinations: Try the split combinations given under floor exercise. With a slight modification, most of them can be executed on the beam. Doing splits on the beam requires more hip flexibility than doing them on the floor. Are you flexible enough to try them?

2h. Mounting means getting on to the beam in order to start a routine. A mount should be a definite move by itself, no matter how simple.

Simple support mounts: Place both hands on the beam and jump up to support. Swing one leg over into straddle sitting position, and use your imagination from there. Or—jump to support, lift one knee on to the beam and turn into the knee scale position.

Vaulting mounts: Use the Reuther board and mount the beam by executing a squat, straddle or wolf vault on to the beam. For skill explanations, refer to vaulting. The spotter should stand in front of the beam, facing the vaulter, and steady her by taking hold of the upper arms.

For vaulting mounts, the board is generally placed fairly close to the beam and the run is short, since the object is to land on the beam and not to vault over it.

Leaping mounts: Use the Reuther board again, and leap into a one-foot stand either on the end or in the middle (crosswise) of the beam. The other foot and arms can be in any desired position. Experiment and see which one you like best (leg in front, in back, to the side; arms up, down, diagonal). Practice this mount on the low beam at first. The board is a little further out than in vaulting mounts, but the run is not much longer. Take-off is from one foot, and your hands never touch the beam.

The spotter should stand next to the beam and extend a hand which the performer can grab if she loses her balance.

Wolf Mount   Leap to the End   Straddle Support

Figure 23. Mounts

Here are some more advanced support mounts:

Straddle support: Approach the beam as in a straddle mount, but place your hands on the beam and lift the hips high so that the straddled legs come over without touching the beam. You are now supporting yourself on your hands, with your legs held in a straddled pike position off the beam. Execute a ¼ turn on your hands, place buttocks on the beam, go into a V-sit, and use your imagination from there.

How many other ways can you mount the beam?

2i. Dismounting is a way of leaving the beam at the end of the routine.

Front rest dismount: From a front leaning rest position on the beam (push-up position), swing one leg down forward, then up backward. Join the other to it by pushing off the beam. From this high front support position, snap down and land sideways to the beam.

Cartwheel to handstand, snap down: Cartwheel to a handstand on the beam, being slightly underbalanced. Snap down, ending up facing the beam.

Cartwheel off the end: Cartwheel to a handstand at the end of the beam. Bring your legs together in the air and continue moving sideways off the beam. Keep your elbows straight and take the hands off one at a time as your body weight passes over them. Land sideways to the end of the beam.

The spotter steadies the performer's upper arms and lets them go one at a time, as the performer takes her hands off the beam.

English handstand archover: Execute an English handstand at the end of the beam. Hold it for a second, then let your legs ride overhead. Arch your upper back and push off the beam, landing with your back to it.

The spotters should stand on the floor at the end of the beam, one on either side. They should each place one hand on the performer's upper arm (thumbs out) and with the other reach out for her upper back, supporting it on the way down.

This is by no means a complete listing of beam skills, but it should give a beginner something to work on. Experiment with other kinds of ideas, then turn to reference books in girls' gymnastics (several are listed in Concept VII).

3. Vaulting is one of the least understood of the girls' events.

Since the entire event consists of only one move (vaulting from a Reuther board over a horse), and since, for the maximum execution of the vault, everything has to be just about perfect (nothing can be covered up or pulled through), the understanding of mechanical principles involved is very important. Once they are understood and mastered, the learning of any vault will become much easier.

3a. First and foremost, the performer has to be able to run.

By this is meant *sprint* running. Too many girls run on their heels, wiggle their hips in the process or use an extremely inefficient arm motion. Space does not permit details about the most efficient running technique. A good high school or college track coach can help a great deal in analyzing the performer's running style. A few general hints for the beginner are:

Run on your toes, with the body leaning slightly forward. Lift up the knees in front, pushing the floor back with the balls of your feet as your weight passes over them. Your arms should be slightly bent at the elbows, swinging forward and back parallel to the body—not crosswise or diagonally. The length of the run is optional, depending on the vault to be executed and on the speed of acceleration. By the end of the run, you should be moving at, or close to, your maximum speed.

Watch the board during the run. The horse is not going to move, as far as the board is concerned, but your run might vary slightly from trial to trial. Watching the board gives you a chance to make small adjustments along the way. If the adjustments have to be major, experiment by shifting your starting point back and forth. A good vaulter should be able to depend on the consistency of her run and concentrate on the execution of the vault at hand. During the last step before the hurdle, shift your focus from the board to the horse.

3b. The hurdle is a way of contacting the board for take-off.

The last running step should be taken on the floor in front of the board. Bring the back leg next to the front one and land on the board with both feet at the same time. This is called the *hurdle*. The hurdle should be low and relatively long, not short and high, as off a diving board. The diver has a flexible board and wants to depress it as much as possible by having her weight fall from a greater distance. But the Reuther board used for vaulting has only very little "give," and the take-off should be accomplished by a quick ankle action upon landing on the board. Land with the weight on the balls of your feet, in about the middle of the board, and take off with a quick ankle push.

Remember—*the hurdle should be low and relatively long*. The longer and faster the run, the further back from the board the last step should be. Do not lift your knee too high in the hurdle; this can cause you to come crashing down onto the board and ruin a quick take-off.

> *3c. Newton's first law of motion states that a body in motion will keep its state and direction until acted upon by an outside force.* The running gymnast is in forward motion and will keep moving in that direction until she herself creates an upward force to partially overcome it, resulting in the body raising up and going over the horse. The hurdle and the *block* are used to convert part of the forward momentum into upward momentum.

During the hurdle, the girl's center of gravity (hips) is still moving forward as a result of the speed created by her run. If nothing is done, by the time she pushes off the board her center of gravity will be so far ahead of her toes that she will leave the board with a definite forward lean; her speed will then take her in a low diagonal flight right *into* the horse, not over it. To avoid this, a beginner is apt to slow down her run by not going all out, and as a result her entire vault will suffer.

At this point, the "block" comes into use. After the last step (in front of the board), the performer should reach forward with both legs and contact the board with her center of gravity BEHIND the base of support (balls of her feet)—not over it. Now, by the time she pushes off the board, her center of gravity will have moved over, not in front of, her toes. As a result, she will leave the board with her center of gravity traveling in a much higher diagonal path and will achieve a nice, high pre-flight before getting on the horse.

Remember—lean back slightly as the knee is brought forward into the hurdle, reach forward with both feet to contact the board, with the toes ahead of the center of gravity, and push off with a quick ankle action. This happens so fast that there is no time to think about all these cues while performing the hurdle. Take them one at a time and repeat the skill using a simple vault you do not have to worry about, until these points during the run and take-off become almost automatic.

3d. There are several theories about the best arm action during the hurdle and take-off. Should a girl reach forward-upward or move her arms to an overhead position from the sides? A beginning vaulter has too much to remember without worrying about the arm action at this stage. As long as the arms get to the forward-upward position by the time she takes off from the board and as long as the arm action does not cause her to lean forward from the hips upon taking off, she is on the right track. Analyzing movies of the best vaulters in the world shows that even high level performers do not use similar arm actions. As long as the arm action does not hinder the vault, use whatever is most convenient for you.

The take-off position is another story. It should be understood and attempted until it becomes a habit. The biggest mistake upon take-off is leaning toward the horse. Even if the hurdle is executed correctly, many girls tend to lean their upper body forward by bending at the hips at the moment they leave the board. A good hurdle and block become almost useless if you take off with a bend at the hips, and with the arms reaching straight for the horse. In order for the center of gravity to stay over the balls of the feet during take-off, the body and legs should be held relatively straight, with the arms reaching forward-upward in front of your face.

LEARNING EXPERIENCE–TAKE-OFF POSITION
Stand on the Reuther board in the take-off position, hips over feet, your upper back slightly rounded, with arms reaching forward-upward. The only bend in the body comes from right under the ribcage, with the diaphragm pulled in (inhale sharply during actual take-off), and from the slightly rounded upper back. This is your take-off position. After leaving the board, you should FOLLOW YOUR ARMS forward-upward off the board and on to the horse, with your hips rising up higher than your head behind you.

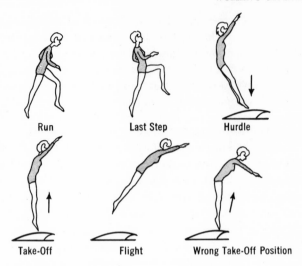

Run   Last Step   Hurdle

Take-Off   Flight   Wrong Take-Off Position

Figure 24.   Vaulting

***3e. As soon as the hands contact the horse, you will be
pushing off again (afterflight).*** Your legs and body should
now be in the correct position for that particular vault. Use the
horse to propel your upper body forward-upward—do not lean on
it. The hands should not rest on the horse, and the push for the
afterflight should be in the upward direction. (For maximum results, the push should be executed while your body is still rising,
not on the way down.) The body straightens during the afterflight,
and then bends at the hips for landing. Land on the balls of
your feet first, let heels go down and sink only into a semi-squat
position. Arms over head or out to the sides, eyes focusing on the
wall ahead of you.

Since the horse is used only for a push in order to give additional flight to the body, practice the run and approach with a
simple vault which does not require a prolonged support on the
hands. A squat vault seems to be the best, since you can land
easily on the horse if something goes wrong in the process and
you do not have sufficient force to go over. Flank, wolf and other
beginning vaults are less suitable, since they require a slightly
longer support position on the horse, which could become an undesirable habit during vaults not needing it. These vaults can be

useful when you are first learning to go over the horse and are hesitant to run fast. Once the basic ideas of vaulting have been mastered, switch to the squat vault and start working on all points covered above. For awhile the vault itself will be second-ary to the run, hurdle, block, take-off and afterflight. Once these skills have been mastered (do not get discouraged; it might take awhile), you are ready to progress into the field of straight-body-ascent vaults discussed later in this concept.

3f. Since the descriptions of basic vaults are available in almost any book of beginning gymnastics, only a selected few are discussed here.

LEARNING EXPERIENCE—SQUAT VAULT

In the basic squat vault, you go over the horse in a tuck position after pushing off with the arms, making certain not to use a prolonged lean on the horse. One or two spotters should stand on the far side of the horse, taking hold of your upper arm(s) with both hands when you place your hands on the horse, and should assist you during the after-flight. The spotters should move with the performer during her off-flight by taking a step or two in the direction of the vault in order not to hold her back.

After you can execute a squat vault comfortably with spotters as well as without, start concentrating on the run and take-off. Move the board back from the horse (at least two or three feet to start with), take a longer and faster run, lean back during the hurdle, reach forward with both legs, push off the board quickly while driving the arms upward and forward, contact the horse as early as possible (while your center of gravity is still moving upward), push off and land. Re-peat the whole process several times, since there is so much to think about. Try to concentrate on a different cue each time, but execute all the other parts of the skill as well as you can. Move the board back gradually as the speed of your run increases, but not to the point where you have to lean forward upon take-off in order to make it to the horse. You can probably vault successfully from a much further dis-tance than you think. Just increase the speed of the run, and keep your body straight during the take-off. Remember to watch the board during the run, shifting your focus to the horse during the last step before the hurdle.

Have another gymnast watch you from the side and critique your take-off position. Is your body straight, with a slightly rounded upper back, and are you driving your body upward off the board, as con-

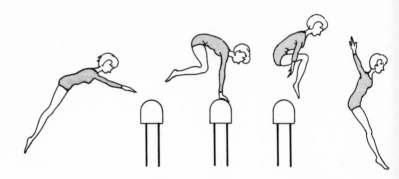

Figure 25.   Squat Vault

trasted to forward into the horse? Do your feet leave the board before your hands touch the horse? Is there an audible pause between hitting the board and hitting the horse? How far can you land in the after-flight?

Straddle vault: The approach and take-off are similar to the squat vault discussed above, except that your hips should rise high off the board and your legs start to straddle. The moment your hands hit the horse, the hips should be at least as high as the shoulders, with legs in a piked straddle position. Push off the horse, bring legs together, and land. The body straightens during the after-flight, then bends at the hips to facilitate landing.

Remember—the hips are as high as the shoulders in this vault. Girls who can execute loose splits have a tendency to tuck their hips under (lower than their shoulders) and go over the horse by practically executing a side split. This is a bad habit to acquire, and should be broken as early as possible.

The spotter (only one is needed here) should stand in back of the horse in a stride standing position (one foot in front of the other). She takes hold of the performer's upper arms and assists her over the horse by stepping back herself in order to make room for the afterflight. Later the spotter should stand further back, ready to step forward and assist if the performer's

Figure 26.   Straddle Vault

feet should hit the horse. She should step back out of the way if her assistance is not needed.

Layout vaulting (straight body ascent): The layout squat is easiest to work with, and also easiest to spot. It is therefore recommended for learning the straight-body-ascent techniques, unless an experienced coach or spotter is readily available and prefers another method.

In a layout vault, the straight body should rise to a horizontal position or above by the time the performer's hands contact the horse. The rest of the vault is executed from there.

Almost every gymnastics coach or teacher dealing with straight-body-ascent vaulting has his or her pet method for getting the girls into layout position. Here are some that this author has found successful:

Two-horse method: Use two side horses, one in front of the other, with the first horse slightly lower, so that the second one can be seen from the starting point. Have the girls vault over the horses, placing their hands on the second horse. Move the horses gradually further apart, and emphasize stretching over the first horse in order to contact the second one with the body horizontal or above. Spot closely at first, using the same method as in a squat vault.

Rope method: Have two girls hold a rope across the path of the runner. The rope should be held parallel to the horse, between the horse and the board. For initial trials, it should be lower than the horse. The girls holding the rope should let it rest loosely on the fingers of the hand toward the vaulter, so it can be pulled down with very little effort if the performer happens to hit it with any part of her body. Move the rope gradually higher and away from the horse. Spot closely at first.

Trampoline method: Place the board in front of the trampoline (without using the horse) and have the girls vault into a dive forward roll on the bed of the trampoline. Emphasize the layout position during the dive. The only way to spot this is to remove a couple of springs from the trampoline and stand between the rim and the bed. Tap the girl slightly under the center of gravity as she flies over your head.

Keep in mind that almost every performer will go through a temporary regression when the extra obstacle is removed. For example, a girl doing beautiful layout squat vaults over two horses will probably regress at first when the other horse is removed. The effect, however, should be temporary and should disappear with continuing practice. Pay special attention to all aspects of the run and take-off during this period. Have the girl *imagine* the extra obstacle and try to achieve the same feeling (kinesthetic sense) she had when it was actually there.

These are by no means the only methods of working for a layout, but they are the ones which can be more readily executed with inexperienced spotters. Since this book is primarily meant for self-teaching purposes, with or without a coach, these three were chosen for presentation.

For variations: execute a layout straddle, a layout stoop (like a squat, but with straight knees, which necessitates an extra lift at the hips). A high layout can easily be converted into a handspring, but a handspring is beyond the scope of this book in its present form.

> *3g. Like a long (broad) jumper in track and field, a vaulter past the beginning stages should start measuring out her run.* The right starting point is at first obtained by trial and error. Once you find it, measure its distance from the board. Use a tape measure, or simply count how many times you can put one

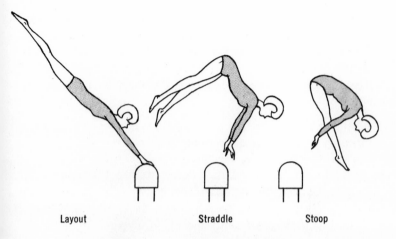

Layout   Straddle   Stoop

Figure 27.   Basic Layout Positions

foot in front of the other in order to cover the distance. Use the same distance when vaulting the next time, and keep using it as long as it feels comfortable. As your skill increases, some adjustments in the length of your run may have to be made, but eventually you should be able to settle for one measurement and use it every time. Different vaults may require different starting points, depending on how much run is needed, but keep the starting point for the same vault constant from practice to practice by measuring it out after you have completed your warm-up vaults. The first warm-up vaults, by the way, should be simple ones. Many competitors use the basic squat for their first few attempts.

Another distance you should measure and become familiar with is the distance of the board from the horse. This may vary for different vaults, depending on the preflight needed and the speed of the run, but make every effort to keep it constant for the same vault from practice to practice. The best distance for the board is also found at first by trial and error. Once found, walk it out by placing one foot in front of the other, and remember the count.

These precautions will enable you to be more consistent in your vaulting. You can stop worrying about hitting the board with the wrong foot (although it sometimes still happens, regardless of everything), or not knowing exactly how far the horse is from the board. This confidence will let you concentrate on the vault itself, and you will end up with much better results.

4. Uneven parallel bars are one of the most challenging and exciting of girls' events.

The ratio of arm strength to body weight is crucial here; hence, a good conditioning program is doubly important.

The next step is to review the movement principles involved in hanging and circling skills. (Refer back to Concept III for principles involved in hanging and swinging.) Attempt once again the learning experiences associated with these skills. Try to feel and understand the movement concepts involved.

Since every move on the uneven bars involves a grip of one kind or another, here are the most commonly used ones:

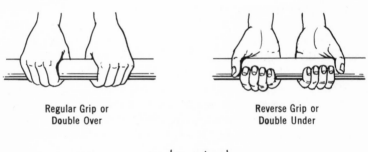

Regular Grip or
Double Over

Reverse Grip or
Double Under

Mixed Grip

Figure 28.   Grips

4a. The basic types of movements for the beginner on the uneven bars are: a) support, b) hang and swing, and c) rotation. Again, refer back to Concept III for ideas and clarification. How many ways can you support yourself on the low bar? On the high bar? How many ways of hanging are there? What about rotation, forward as well as backward? Many teachers of beginning gymnastics advocate the exploratory approach at first, in order for the girls to gain confidence and become used to the equipment. Use of the bars is also an interesting way to build arm strength.

LEARNING EXPERIENCE—EXPLORATORY ROUTINE I
Only a broad outline of a possible exploratory routine is presented here. No details are given. Fill in the gaps, getting into positions and changing them any way you wish.

Climb or jump to support on the low bar—any way you want. Change your position to a hang from the high bar, using your imagination to get there smoothly. Turn to face the low bar, and swing or lift your legs over it to a sitting position. Find a way to get to a front support position on the high bar, facing the low bar. Rotate around the high bar, ending up sitting on the low bar. Dismount from the low bar.

Repeat this routine with different combinations. Do not be concerned with the "right way of doing things" at this time. Just explore and get the feel of the bars, even if you feel like a monkey climbing trees or a small child frolicking on the playground (after all, that is where many ideas originally came from).

Some basic uneven bar moves in the three categories stated at the beginning of this concept are:

a) Support:

Front support: Stand in front of both bars, facing them, and place your hands on the low bar, using the overgrip. Jump to a straight arm support. Lean slightly forward, taking some of the weight on your thighs. Body straight, head in line with the body, slight arch in upper back, legs together, with the toes pointed.

Rear support: Get to a sitting position on the low bar, hands next to hips, with an overgrip. Lean slightly back from the upper body. Straighten arms and let them support some of your body weight. Keep your feet together, toes pointing toward the floor, upper body slightly arched, head in line with the body.

Stride support: Sit with one leg in front and the other in back of the low bar. Arms next to hips, with an undergrip (thumbs

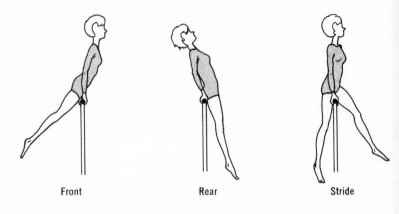

Front   Rear   Stride

Figure 29.   Supports

forward). Body upright, knees straight and toes pointed, head in
lie with the body. Keep your hips between the hands (not in back
of the hands) and take some body weight on the arms.

   b) Ways of hanging:

Long hang: Jump to hang from the high bar, using the overgrip.
(Review the hanging procedures explained in Concept III.)

Pike inverted hang: Hang from the low bar, bring legs up between arms and straighten them out parallel to the floor. Look at
the ceiling through the knees and find a point of balance. An
overgrip or undergrip can be used, depending on the direction of
movement from that point.

Knee hang: Climb to a knee hang from the low bar. Let go with
the arms and straighten them out to the sides. Look down at the
mat, body straight from the knees down.

   c) Rotation:

Forward roll (Front support to hang or dismount): Jump to a
front support on the low bar, with your hands in an overgrip.
Bend forward at the hips (hands shift further around the bar),
tuck, rotate around the bar in the forward direction and drop
your legs slowly to the ground.

Backward roll (Rear support to stand on the floor): Rear support on the low bar, hands in the overgrip position. Lean slightly forward from the waist and slide the bar down to the knees. Rotate backward to pike inverted hang position, and continue bringing your legs over head until they touch the mat. Release the bar, and stand up.

LEARNING EXPERIENCE—EXPLORATORY ROUTINE II
This is another outline of a possible routine. This time the directions are a little more specific, taking into account moves explained above. Getting from position to position, however, is still left up to the imagination of the student.

Jump to front support on the low bar, facing the high bar. Lift your legs over the low bar one at a time, simultaneously transferring hands from LB to HB. Drop to a hang from the high bar. Turn around in the hanging position (through a mixed grip), and lift your legs over the low bar to rear support. Your hands remain on the high bar. Twist to one side (either one) and stand up on the low bar, facing the high bar. Execute a forward roll over the high bar to a long hang position. Swing backward and forward, jumping off on the front swing.

---

d) Other basic rotational movements:

"Skin the cat": Stand on the low bar, facing the high bar. Your hands should be on the high bar, in an overgrip. Lift one leg over the high bar (between your hands) and drop to a single knee hang. Your hands stay on the high bar. Bring the other leg over the high bar also, straightening to a pike inverted hang. Execute a backward roll until your toes touch the low bar. Slide your legs down along the low bar until your body is straight. Keep your head up. Let go of the high bar with one hand, and rotate into a side sitting position on the low bar.

Kickover hip circle, low bar: Stand in front of the low bar, your hands resting on it with an overgrip, elbows bent. Take one step forward in order to bring the hips under the bar, then kick forward-upward with the other leg, leaning back at the shoulders and straightening the arms *slightly*. When your shoulders get under the bar, pull with your arms in order to bring the bar into the bending point of your hips. Keep your legs rotating around the bar. Straighten the body to the front support position.

Here are a few suggestions helpful for the beginner: keep the elbows bent during the first half of the move. Beginners tend to straighten the elbows too soon and let the hips drop under the bar. Look at your feet coming up, before straightening your arms and leaning back from the shoulders. DO NOT THROW THE HEAD BACK during the rotation; it should stay in line with the body. The spotter or spotters should stand between the bars, facing each other, with the performer between them. After the performer has kicked off the ground, they should place their hands under her buttocks and assist in bringing her hips up to the bar. They should then assist her with the rotation.

Kickover hip circle, high bar: Assume a rear support position on the low bar, with your hands in an overgrip on the high bar. Bend one knee and place the ball of the foot on the low bar, with your hips resting over the heel. The other foot stays in extended position over the low bar. Your hips are fully extended. Look at the high bar and bend your elbows slightly. From this position, push your hips up by straightening the bent leg and kick with the straight leg into a circle around the high bar. Bring legs together and rotate backward into a front support position on the high bar. Please note—*the push-kick is one continuous action, not two separate movements.* Look at your feet coming up, then lean

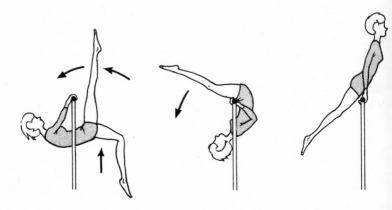

Figure 30. Kickover Hip Circle

back from the shoulders and straighten arms, then pull the bar into the bending point of the hips. Do not throw your head back; it stays in line with the body.

The spotter or spotters stand between the bars, facing each other, with the performer between them. One hand goes under the performer's seat, the other under her shoulders. As the performer leaves the low bar, they assist her hips upward. Once her hips are out of reach, they can exert upward push at the shoulder. For younger age-groups, both bars could be lowered for teaching purposes. In this way, even the short spotter can be of help until the performer masters the skill by herself.

Forward hip circle: Start from the front support position on the low bar, facing out. Arch your body and push the bar three or four inches down the thighs. In that position, let yourself fall forward, rotating in a straight body position around the bar until your body is parallel to the floor. At this point, pike hard from the upper body, getting as close to your knees as possible. Now shift the overgrip to the top of the bar and rotate back up.

Keep in mind that the most common mistake is piking too early at the beginning of the move, before the body has reached the horizontal position. The result is a pike forward roll off the bar. The momentum for this skill has to be started with a

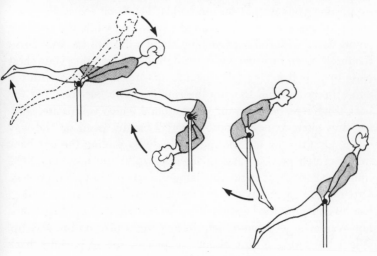

Figure 31.   Forward Hip Circle

straight body fall. Yes, it is unsettling at first to fall forward with nothing in front of you, but keep trying, delaying the piking action a little more each time until you get to the horizontal position. After a fast piking action, stay in that position until your shoulders get back up over the bar, then push into a front support position.

The spotter stands between the bars, facing the performer. She puts her hand closest to the low bar under the bar, around it and on top of the performer's seat. She should go with the performer, without exerting any pressure during the falling phase of the move, then press the performer's center of gravity close to the bar. The spotter should put her other hand on the performer's upper back on the way up and help with rotation. Please note that, on the way down during this move, the body has been lengthened (by moving the bar down the thighs) in order for the gravity to act on a larger mass and start a fast rotation. On the way up, when gravity works against the move, the body is shortened by piking. The result is increased rotation which overcomes gravity's action and helps to complete the move.

Split circle: Start with a stride support position on the low bar, hands in an undergrip. Body straight, head held in line with body (do not bend forward or look down). Lift your body off the bar, supporting your weight on the hands. The front leg is stretched and lifted up as close to horizontal as possible, while the back leg points down with the bar touching about a third of the way down the thigh. Lean forward with a straight body, bringing your chest close to your front leg (the head is up), reach forward with the entire body and fall to start the rotation. The bar touching the back thigh now becomes the point around which you rotate. Having thus elongated the body, you will create speed on the way down. On the way up, shorten the body by pulling the bar back to the crotch position and piking *slightly* at the hips. Do NOT round your back or bend your elbows excessively in the process. Experienced gymnasts can get back up with little or no piking, just by changing the location of the bar on the way up. Beginners, however, will get definite help from a *slight* pike on the way up. When the circle is just about completed, the grip shifts back to the top of the bar and the legs can be brought together in order to make getting up easier.

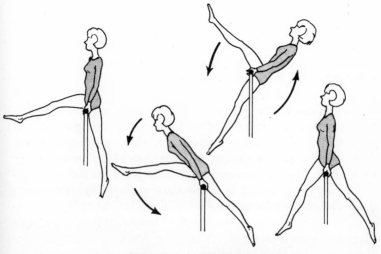

Figure 32.   Split Circle

Here are some helpful suggestions—the most common mistakes a beginner makes are not elongating the body enough on the way down (rounding her back, pulling her head forward, or even piking at her hips instead of extending), or using too much pike to get back up. The tendency is to round the back on the way up, to bring the head forward and to bend at the elbows, which will result in the performer losing all the rotational speed and falling back to a single knee hang. A beginner may benefit from bringing the legs as close together as possible half way through the circle, and leaving them that way.

The spotter or spotters should stand between the bars, facing the performer between them (the performer, in this example, is facing out on the low bar). Each should take her hand closest to the low bar, bring it under the bar and around, taking hold of the performer's wrist with a rotated grasp. The spotters should go with the performer on the way down, then exert pressure with their other hands under her upper back on her way up.

4b. A cast, in simplified terms, involves moving the body in one direction in order to prepare for a movement in another direction. It could be compared to cocking a pistol or pulling back the bowstring in preparation for shooting an arrow.

Casting moves are very important basic skills on the uneven parallel bars. They are needed to:

1. change position on a single bar
2. provide take-off for more advanced moves

Though casting moves may look deceptively easy for a novice, many girls and coaches find them troublesome, and are liable to jump over this very important step in developing uneven bar skills. This omission will show up very soon in the quality of the work shown by the performer, hindering her further development. This point cannot be emphasized strongly enough—*understand the mechanical principles involved in casting moves and keep working on them,* even though they may seem too simple to be worth the trouble.

As far as the direction of the move is concerned, casts can be divided into the following categories:

a. Support casts
b. Under bar casts

a. Support casts:

Cast back to the bar: Jump to front support position on the low bar, with your hands in an overgrip. Bend the elbows enough to bring the bar to the bending point of your hips. Simultaneously dip your shoulders forward and swing the legs under the bar to pike position, with the center of gravity remaining over the bar. From the low point of this dip, swing the legs back up and extend the arms forcefully. The point of rotation during the upswing is at the shoulders. The rest of the body should raise up perfectly straight (no arch), with the head in line with the body (not thrown back). Work up to the horizontal position at the top of your cast. Following a moment of weightlessness at the top of the swing, the body will drop back to the bar, bending at the hips upon contact to minimize the impact of landing.

Here are some things to remember—shoulders should stay forward during the entire move. Keeping the eyes focused on the floor in front of the bars can help to avoid unnecessary head movements, since there is a tendency (for a beginner) to throw her head back while casting away from the bar. Since the entire move should be executed IN BALANCE (there should be no feeling of falling backward or forward), the center of gravity should stay over the base of support, as indicated in Fig. 33.

Once the basic cast has been mastered, start working on the variations. Execute the cast once more and concentrate on the timing of the body. Feel the raising off the bar, the moment of weightlessness and coming back down. Try to anticipate these points of movement.

Cast single leg shoot through: Cast off the bar. Just before reaching the top of your swing (the hips are still moving up), round your back, pull one knee to the chest and bring the leg between the arms over the bar. Straighten the body during the downswing and end in a stride support position.

Here are some helpful suggestions—your shoulders should stay forward during the first part of the move. As the leg moves toward the bar, shoulders start moving back, ending over the base of support (the bar) in the final position. Your head stays in line with the body, looking up at the end of the move. Round your back and push down on the bar while bringing the leg through.

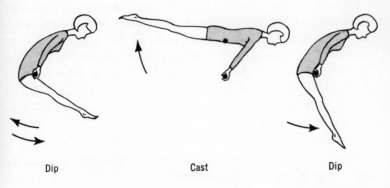

Dip   Cast   Dip

Figure 33.   Cast

Since the move happens too fast in order for most beginners to react to all the cues, a spotter can slow down the lowering phase of the move so that the performer has time to get her leg through. The spotter should stand between the bars, facing the performer, on the side of the leg that will remain straight. During the cast, she puts one hand under the performer's thigh (palm up) and slows down her descent. Her other hand can go under the bar and up in order to steady the performer's upper arm.

Cast to stand: At the top of the cast, while the hips are still moving upward, round your back and bring both knees to the chest, placing the balls of the feet on the bar between the hands.

Concentrate on the following cues: push down on the bar while pulling the knees to the chest. Focus your eyes low on the mat in front of the bars, since a high head position will prevent effective rounding of the back. Shoulders are in front of the bar during the upswing, moving slowly back when the legs are brought in, and ending up just slightly in front of the base of support (the hands) for better balance. If they stay too far back or move too far forward, you will lose your balance in the squat position. After being able to land in a balanced position, practice standing up on the bar at the end of the move.

Cast double leg shoot through (cast squat-through). This is done the same as a cast to a stand—except, instead of placing your feet on the bar, bring both feet through between your hands and end in a rear support position on the low bar.

Here are some important points: the interplay of legs and shoulders is the key to success here. During the first half of the move the shoulders are forward, as in all the casting moves. As legs come in, shoulders start moving back over the bar, ending up slightly behind the bar when legs are straightened and lowered in front. Head stays low until the legs are through and the body is straightening up. Look forward-upward at the conclusion of the move.

The key word in all these position-changing cast moves is *balance.* Keep the center of gravity (somewhere around the hips, depending on body position) over the base of support (hands on the bar). When one part of the body moves in front

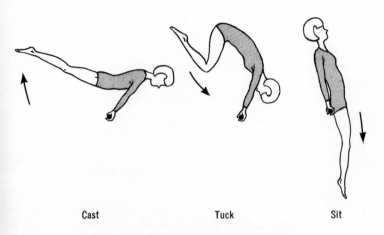

Cast   Tuck   Sit

Figure 34.   Cast Double Leg Shoot Through

of the bar, another has to move in back of it (and the other way around) in order to keep balance.

Cast to backward hip circle: Cast off the bar with straight body, shoulders forward, hips over hands. Come down with a straight body also—but the moment you feel the slightest pressure of the bar at the hips, lean back from the shoulders and follow your legs in a backward hip circle around the bar. Beginners can bend slightly at the hips while going around, but more advanced girls should be able to execute the move with an almost straight body, leaning back just before their hips hit the bar. End up in a front support position at the end of the circle, and do not let your legs swing under the bar from there. You can try to prevent this by pushing the bar one or two inches down your thighs at the end of the circle, simultaneously resisting the piking action of the hips by tightening up the muscles in the lower back.

Note the following thing: *head position is important here—* keep it in line with the body and do not try to initiate the circling action by throwing your head back. Timing is important also. Beginners can lean back at the shoulders the very moment they feel the hips getting back to the bar. More advanced girls should lean back a split second before. But remember—leaning back too early will result in falling off the bar. On the other hand, waiting too long or piking the hips before they reach the bar will kill the rotational force, making it impossible to get a smooth rotation, if any at all.

The spotter should stand between the bars, facing the performer. (The performer is facing out.) She should place her hand closest to the high bar on the back of the performer's hips as the performer is coming down, pressing the performer's center of gravity close to the bar. Her other hand can assist in the circling action of the performer's legs.

Cast off the bar: Here the object is to get the center of gravity off the bar in a controlled fashion. Try it on the low bar first.

From a front support on the low bar, dip, cast your hips up and away from the bar, push away with hands, let go and jump to a stand behind the bar. Repeat the move again, concentrating on the following points:

a) Do not arch; keep your body straight. Your shoulders, hips and heels should be in line with each other.
b) Look down in front of the bars, so that your head stays in line with your body. See the bar go past your face.
c) As a beginner, do not attempt to raise your shoulders above the bar and cast away with straight arms, as you may have seen world champions do. The straight-arm cast belongs to a more advanced performer. Bend your elbows and bring the bar past your face before releasing it.

After feeling comfortable with the cast off the low bar, attempt it off the high bar. Now you will not release the bar, but end up in a long hang position under the bars. A spotter is needed at this point, to keep you from swinging into the low bar.

Start in a front support position on the high bar, facing the low bar. Dip, cast your hips away from the bar (with bent elbows), push the bar away by straightening the arms and swing down with a straight body pendulum swing.

Concentrate on the following: keep the body from arching during the cast. Make sure to bend the elbows and bring the bar past close to your face. Do not attempt to cast too high on the high bar as a beginner; otherwise, you will have trouble controlling the speed of the move. A diagonally downward direc tion is ample at first, but be sure to push away from the bar and get your elbows straight before hitting the bottom of the swing.

The spotter stands between the bars, facing the high bar. As the performer nears the bottom of her swing, the spotter grabs her around the hips and slows down the performer's forward momentum.

Cast off the high bar to wrap around or flying hip circle: Execute a controlled cast off the high bar, approaching the low bar with a straight body. As soon as you feel the pressure of the low bar at the hips, pike *slightly* around the bar and go into a backward hip circle, letting go of the high bar with the hands, transferring the grip to the low bar in the process. Try to end up in a front support position without letting your legs swing under the bar from there. (Refer back to stopping a backward hip circle.)

Note: the most common mistakes are coming into the bar with prematurely piked hips, or improper timing of the hand release from the high bar. The body should be kept straight during the swing into the bar, and at the moment of contact the hips should be slightly in front of the heels. From there on, proceed as in a regular backward hip circle. As far as the timing of the release is concerned, wait until you see your legs raising up on the other side of the bar, then transfer. Make sure the transfer is made while the legs are still in motion; do not wait until they lose their swing. As you get more advanced, try to eliminate excessive piking from the move, going around with a minimum of piking action. And remember—it is very important to stop at the end of the circle *without* letting your feet swing under the bar.

Another common mistake in this move is coming to the low bar with a poor cast, with body arched and the heels *way* behind the hips. This will result in an uncontrollably fast circle, and you will most likely not be able to stay on the bar. These mistakes should be corrected right away, before they become a habit, since a wrap around is an important take-off for many advanced moves, which cannot be executed correctly if the wrap around is improperly done.

Spotting is similar to the backward hip circle. The spotter stands between the bars, facing the performer. As the performer swings toward the bar, the spotter places one hand behind the performer's hips, keeping them close to the bar. With the other, she helps the rotation of the performer's legs.

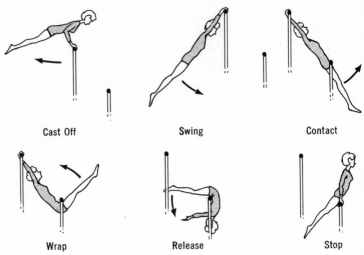

Cast Off   Swing   Contact

Wrap   Release   Stop

Figure 35.   Wrap Around Hip Circle

After having mastered the support casts, you can try the following variations and combinations:

a) Cast single leg shoot through to a split circle. This can be executed on the low as well as the high bar.
b) Forward hip circle, cast, backward hip circle. This can also be executed on either bar.
c) Forward hip circle, immediate cast to single leg shoot through, cast to stand or cast double leg shoot through.

b. Under bar casts:
Cast half twist: Start by sitting on the low bar, facing the high bar. Your hands are on the high bar, in a mixed grip, with one hand crossed over the other. Your sitting position should be far enough forward on the bar so that your legs can swing up and down freely without restraint. Arch your body, swinging legs down, then pike and drive straight legs up toward the high bar. In order to do this, you have to straighten the arms and lean back from the shoulders. At this point, your shoulders will be under the bar, with the hips piked and knees almost touching the hands. After the center of gravity passes under the high bar, extend the body forcefully and twist while extending. Come back to the low

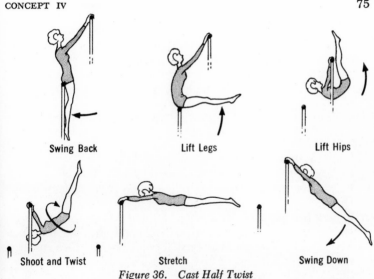

Swing Back   Lift Legs   Lift Hips

Shoot and Twist   Stretch   Swing Down

Figure 36.   Cast Half Twist

bar, facing it with a straight body pendulum swing. Have a spotter stop you there. Later, after mastering the cast half twist, come in to the low bar and execute a backward hip circle.

Here are some helpful suggestions: beginners tend to drop their hips off the low bar in the downward direction, instead of swinging them up and driving their knees to the high bar. This happens if the arms are not straightened during the upswing and there is no leaning back at the shoulders The resulting turn is very slow, and there is no swing left. Drive the knees up, watch the legs start the extension, then turn, initiating the twist with the hips (not with the shoulders). The half twist should be completed before the weightless moment at the top of the swing. From there on, it is a straight body downswing.

It is helpful to the beginner if a spotter stands between the bars and gives an upward boost to the hips after they leave the low bar. The spotter can also assist in rotation and slow down the downswing from the same position.

Here are some variations and combinations:

a) Jump to a front support on the low bar, facing the high bar. Cast squat through to rear support, transfer the hands to the high bar and execute a cast half twist wrap around.

b) From the front support on the low bar, cast to a squat position on the low bar, transfer your hands to the high bar and take off to the cast half twist wrap around from there. Bring your ankles to the high bar, with your knees bent, then straighten your legs into the twist. The rest is the same.

Here are some suggestions for simple mounts and dismounts.

Mounts:
a) Jump to support on the low bar.
b) Kickover hip circle to a front support on the low bar.
c) Facing the low bar, run, jump to a squat position on the low bar.
d) Facing the high bar, run, jump to a hang from the high bar, swing your legs forward, then back and straddle or squat over the low bar on your next forward swing. End up in a rear support, with hands on high bar.
e) Run, jump to a hang from the high bar, swing forward, then back, and execute a wrap around on the low bar at the end of the second forward swing. A more difficult variation is to go directly into the wraparound from your first forward swing.
f) From standing under the bars, jump to a hang from the high bar, facing out, with your hands in an overgrip. Execute a beat swing (refer to Concept III). As you go into the pike, pull knees up to the chest and continue them through the hands to a skin the cat position. A more difficult variation is to execute a beat swing and continue the pike into a pull over hip circle to the high bar, ending in a front support on the high bar, facing out.

Dismounts:
a) Backward roll off the low bar.
b) Forward roll over the high bar to long hang, and drop off. For a variation, swing forward and back in the long hang position; during the second forward swing, jump off with a half turn right or left.
c) From front support on the low bar, facing out, cast, pull the knees to the chest and execute a squat vault over the low bar. For a variation, cast into a straddle or flank vault over the low bar. Spot as in vaulting.
d) From front support on the high bar, facing in, drop backward to a piked hang (knees touching the bar). As the body swings

forward, extend the hips to an arched position and thrust the
bar behind the head. Pass over the low bar and land in front
of it.

After having mastered the circling and casting moves, you
are ready to move on to kipping moves, bar-to-bar changes and
other combinations which are beyond the scope of this book at
its present stage. There are many excellent books available—
several listed in Concept VII—to which you may turn for further
help.

Please remember this also—uneven bar work, from here on,
should be executed under the guidance of a teacher, coach or
more advanced person, who can help to interpret the source
materials as well as correct mistakes in technique and execution.
Competent spotting during the first few trials becomes more and
more important. Although the basic skills up to this point can
be attempted by working in small groups and spotting each
other as described in this book, self-study from here on can result
in wasted time through costly mistakes and the acquiring of bad
working habits. If this book has aroused your interest in gymnastics and given you a small start, it has served its purpose;
from here on, search for outside help and guidance.

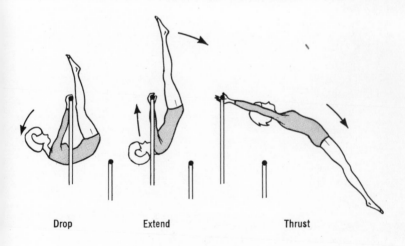

Drop   Extend   Thrust

Figure 37.   Dismount

Outcomes

After working on this concept, you should be able to:

1. Make up a simple floor exercise routine and draw a floor pattern for it.

2. Be able to execute at least two different rolls, turns, leaps, poses and one inverted support or handstand combination. The last move could be done with a spotter.

3. Make up a balance beam routine and execute it on the beam or on the floor, depending on your personal skill at the time.

4. Spot simple rolls on the balance beam.

5. Execute at least one basic vault, and know the mistakes you tend to make in the run, hurdle, blocking and take-off positions.

6. Analyze these skills for a friend.

7. List the grips used on the uneven bars, and name at least one move using each.

8. Demonstrate the basic support positions on the uneven bars.

9. Spot a friend in two basic circling movements around the bar.

10. Analyze the relationship of center of gravity to the base of support in basic casting moves.

11. Execute a simple mount and dismount on the uneven parallel bars.

Concept V—The Rules of the Activity Can Depend Almost Entirely on the Objectives of the Participant

As INDICATED IN Concept I, gymnastics activities cover a wide area of interests and abilities. If you are participating in gymnastics just for your own enjoyment and exercise, no specific rules apart from safety precautions are necessary.

If your objective is to perform at demonstrations or gymnastics shows, use good sense plus good showmanship. Here are a few suggestions:

a) Use short, lively and interesting routines well within the capabilities of the participants. There is nothing worse than making the audience suffer with a weak performer—keeping their fingers crossed that she will be able to get through without a mishap.
b) Use your imagination and come up with something slightly different. How about two girls performing a synchronized routine on the balance beam? Could the same thing be done on uneven parallel bars? Group routines in floor exercise can be fascinating, especially when small hand apparatus is used (balls, Indian clubs, hoops). How about mixing group and individual numbers in one big presentation with a central theme?
c) Make use of background music and colored lights, but always be sure that the safety of the performer comes first. For that reason, elaborate costumes are not advisable when performing on the apparatus; use simple versions of the basic leotard.

1. A definite set of rules comes up only if you decide to go into the competitive phase of gymnastics.

Even here, the rules may vary with the level of competition and the sponsoring organization. An effort is being made all over the United States to standardize the rules of competitive gymnastics, basing them on the rulings of the Federation of International Gymnastics (FIG). As the sport grows and changes, FIG keeps modifying the basic rules. Sometimes the changes are minor, sometimes major and far-reaching. For this reason, we will not go into detailed rules and regulations for competitive gymnastics. We will, however, list the basic requirements for each of the four competitive events.

1a. The floor exercise routine should consist of dance, tumbling, acrobatics and gymnastics movements with a liberal use of leaps, jumps, turns and rolls. It should show change of pace, level and quality of movement (mood of the routine). The area (about 40′ × 40′) should be covered in its entirety. A routine should be accompanied by music played by one instrument. The time limit is from one minute to one minute 30 seconds. The newest trends show the appearance of limited modern dance and jazz movements in floor exercise routines, spiced by adaptations of ethnic dance steps. The music is also leaning toward popular and ethnic themes.

1b. The work on the balance beam is getting progressively closer to floor exercise. A routine on the beam should be lively and fast; only three held positions are allowed. Leaps, turns, jumps and rolls should be generously mixed with tumbling and flexibility moves. Changes of level, mood and pace should be evident. The time limit is one minute 20 seconds to one minute 45 seconds, and good performers cover the beam 6–10 times within the time allotted. The trend is to work the beam sideways and diagonally as well as backward and forward.

1c. Hanging and swinging moves should dominate an uneven bar routine. Stops or intermediate swings are out. The routine should be flowing and continuous, and should show work below the low bar and above the high bar as well as between the bars. There is no time limit, but by unofficial agreement a routine should consist of 8 to 12 major parts.

1d. A long preflight, a short but vigorous tap on the horse and a long, high afterflight are the major parts of any vault. The trend is for more height, distance and lively flight over the horse. The landing should be solid, and the entire vault should appear effortless.

Concept VI—Proper Conditioning and Weight Control Are Very Important to a Young Girl Hoping to Achieve Some Degree of Skill in Gymnastics

IT HAS ALWAYS been incomprehensible how so many of us are willing to put our bodies through strenuous physical feats without first preparing or "tuning" our instrument for the task ahead. We take too much for granted, one of the results being the unsafe reputation attached to gymnastics in many parts of the country. Granted, the activity is not "natural" to the soft, overfed and under-exercised human body fast becoming prevalent in our culture today. Yet, it is very natural to the experimental and inquisitive nature of youth. One only has to observe young children of different cultures and backgrounds at play to see many examples of this. It is up to us to train our bodies to do what our minds say they can do.

The preparation of one's body for gymnastics requires special attention to the following areas:

a) weight control
b) strength
c) flexibility
d) endurance

1. Even a moderately overweight girl will have a hard time mastering her body in gymnastics.

We know from physics and anatomy that a human body is composed mostly of third-class levers which favor speed, but we are very inefficient as far as strength is concerned. The amount of extra strength needed to handle an additional pound of body weight is surprising. What about girls who are 5, 10 or 15 pounds over what they should be? Most girls can handle their bodies much better if they lose 5 to 10 pounds, even if they are not overweight according to the most popular weight tables. Put on a leotard and stand in front of a long mirror. Do you look as good as you should? Most fashions today cover up bulging hips, fat

81

waistlines and relaxed abdomens. A leotard covers up nothing. If you decide to become serious about gymnastics, a leotard is the outfit you will be spending a lot of time in and be seen in by a lot of people of both sexes. Is this the image you wish to convey? In most cases, gymnastics alone is not enough to give you a suitable figure; a careful diet has to go along with it. Ninety percent of the top gymnasts diet along with their training in order to look better and gain more body control. The results are well worth it, both esthetically and skillwise.

2. The next step is to start working on your strength, flexibility and endurance.

Strength is most important in arms, hip flexors and abdominal muscles. In flexibility, special attention should be paid to the hips and upper back (shoulder joints).

The last, but by no means least, is endurance—cardiovascular as well as muscular.

Exercises to fit every one of these categories can be found in many books dealing with fitness or body mechanics. Only a few samples of each are given here.

2a. Strength.

Arms—start with modified or "girl's" push-ups, work up to the regular or "boy's" way of executing them. Then increase the number or speed of execution. Work the same way with pull-ups. Here the changeover from modified (girl's type) to regular ones will probably be more difficult, so use an intermediate step. After becoming able to execute a good number of modified pull-ups without undue effort, start by trying the lowering phase of the hanging pull-up. Have someone assist you to the "up" position, then lower slowly to a straight-arm hang. Working with still or traveling rings, horizontal ladders and climbing ropes is another way of increasing arm strength. Try to work up to climbing the rope, using only your hands, as many circus acrobats do.

Abdominals—practice sit-ups of various types. If the main objective is to strengthen abdominals and not necessarily the hip flexors, use a bent knee position. Here are a few unusual sit-ups, after you become able to execute a good number (over 30) of the conventional ones:

Snap-ups: start from a supine position, arms along the sides. Snap to a bent knee V-sit position, bringing your knees to your chest without touching your toes to the floor or helping in any way with your arms. Lower your body back down, keeping your heels 2″ off the floor, and straighten your knees. Make sure to lower your head to the floor, but not your heels. Repeat. Your arms should be inactive during this exercise. It is best to keep them a few inches off the floor, along the sides of your body.

Reach-ups: start again from a supine position, with your arms crossed in front of your chest. Lift your legs up straight to a 45° angle and have a partner hold on to your ankles (she can steady your feet against her body). Now sit up and reach for your knees with your elbows. Lower down and repeat. If the exercise becomes too easy, have your partner steady your legs at a higher angle, up to 90° from the floor.

Hip flexors—hanging leg lifts are one of the best hip flexor exercises. Start in a hanging position, pull your knees up to your chest, hold, lower slowly. After this becomes easy, pull your knees up to your chest, straighten to L position, hold, lower. The last step is to lift your legs with your knees straight to L position, hold, lower slowly. Now try to raise your legs straight beyond the horizontal and touch your toes to the bar. Be sure not to get help from a preliminary swing.

There is nothing wrong with a girl doing strength exercises or working with weights, as long as it is done properly and used as part of a *total* conditioning program. This will keep you slim and muscularly tight. The additional body control will make your work in gymnastics look graceful and effortless, minimizing the chances of injury and greatly increasing the probability of success.

2b. Flexibility. Which one of us has not, at one time or another, envied a girl who can execute splits and backbends with ease? We tend to call her double-jointed. Anatomically, there is no such thing; all normal human beings have the same number of joints. The difference is in the range of motion of these joints, and this can be increased through exercise.

Hip flexibility forward—any form of toe-touching or sitting and reaching in various positions is a good start. To get the most benefit out of the stretch, keep your lower back straight and your head up. A rounded lower back gives only the illusion of being able to reach further or bounce lower, but the stretch on hamstrings is greatly reduced and some acrobatic teachers consider it bad for the lower back. Remember, your chest should touch your knees (or floor) before your head does. Recent findings indicate that sustained pressure in stretching exercises is superior to bouncing.

Ballet stretches—lift one leg up on the balance beam or on some other object, a little higher than your waist. Face the "ballet bar" at first, with your leg straight in front of you, making sure that your hips remain parallel to the bar (there is a great tendency to stand partially turned). Both knees should be straight, and your leg on the bar should be turned out with a strongly-pointed toe. Lift your arms over your head and reach forward with a straight body, head up. Try to put your chest on your thigh. Try the same thing sideways. Your hips should now be at right angles to the bar, and your leg lifted as far to the side as possible (there is a great tendency to turn toward the bar). Lift your arms over your head and lean sideways toward your leg, attempting to rest your ear on your shin. Do not turn toward your leg. Both knees should be straight, your leg on the bar being turned out so that your knee faces the ceiling.

Do not overlook stretches in split position—forward and backward as well as sideways.

Hip flexibility backward—this is the most often neglected area and is the chief reason beginners are unable to do splits. Your lead leg may have enough forward hip flexibility, but your rear leg does not have sufficient backward hip flexibility. If this condition is not understood and remedied, a technically poor split will result, in which the hips are not at right angles to the legs (as shown in Fig. 38). Besides being unattractive, this split will cut down the possibilities of split combinations and will hinder the further development of the gymnast.

Lack of backward hip flexibility comes from overly tight (but not necessarily strong) hip flexors, which need to be stretched. Track coaches have several hip stretching exercises that they use with runners and vaulters; we should adapt them for our purposes.

Here is one used by many gymnastics teachers:

Take a long lunge position. Your rear leg should be straight,

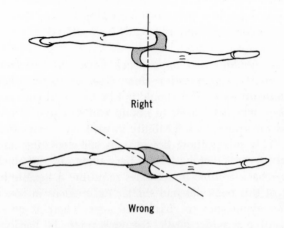

Right

Wrong

Figure 38.   Splits

with your knee facing the floor and your toe curled under. The knee of your front leg should face straight forward. Now go to a deep-knee bend with your front leg, aiming to sit on your heel (your heel is off the floor). Your rear leg remains straight, with no bend at the knee. Your body is in the vertical position, with the hip of your rear leg fully extended (as in Fig. 39).

Figure 39.   Stretching the Hip Flexors

Another way of increasing backward hip flexibility is to lean your body back in a split position, trying to face the ceiling. In this case, a good split should already be mastered.

2c. Shoulder and upper back flexibility is extremely important in gymnastics, since most of the acrobatic work depends on it.

This should not be confused with lower back flexibility, which is easier to obtain and can sometimes be substituted for upper back flexibility in walkovers and other similar stunts. This substitution, however, is self-defeating and is considered by many acrobatics teachers as one of the chief sources of lower back trouble in activities requiring a flexible back. The author of this book has had similar experiences in coaching and teaching gymnastics to girls of all ages. There is no substitute for a flexible shoulder girdle, though it might be harder to attain than any other phase of flexibility, depending on the age and natural stiffness of the student.

Lower the balance beam to waist level, or use something else at that height. Face the beam and place your wrists on it, then back away and lean forward until your back is parallel to the floor, with your hips bent at a 90-degree angle. With your head up, look at the beam. Keep your knees straight, and your legs slightly apart. Have a partner stand next to you and press down with her hands at the convexity of your upper back. Try to keep your lower back flat during this exercise, and do not let your wrists slip off to the front of the beam. Arch only from your upper back region. Backbend exercises are also very beneficial, if done correctly. Push into a backbend from the floor. Straighten your elbows, if you can, and try to bring your shoulders right over your hands. Your knees should be as straight as possible, and your heels on the floor. After this position becomes easy, straighten your knees and push your shoulders out beyond the heels of your hands, arching only from your upper back. Try to lift your head up (putting your chin on your chest) and look at the ceiling. This should be accomplished without any loss of flexibility in your shoulder girdle; otherwise, keep your head back and look at the floor.

Flexibility tends to deteriorate faster than any other phase of body condition, and therefore has to be worked at constantly. Shoulder flexibility is in many cases the first to go, resulting in

Stiff Shoulders   **Good**   **Too Much Arch in
                                                                   the Lower Back**

Figure 40.   Upper Back Flexibility

undesirable substitutions in skills depending on a flexible shoulder girdle. Since flexibility is so important in gymnastics, work at it daily, even if it hurts and the results seem so slow in materializing. Stretching tight muscles may be more uncomfortable than any other phase of conditioning, and therefore the girls who need it most are liable to work least at it. Self-discipline is greatly needed here, particularly since the results may not show as quickly as in other areas.

2d. *Almost every active sport requires endurance, mostly of the cardiovascular type.* Gymnastics requires a high degree of muscular endurance along with it, particularly in the arms and shoulders. The lack of endurance might not show up until you are prepared to put your skills together into a routine for a show or competition, but then it becomes crucial.

Cardiovascular endurance—any form of running, either for distances or in place, is the best exercise here. Sustained skipping, hopping or any similar activity can provide a welcome change of pace. Try it to music with a fast beat, and keep up with the record. Rope-jumping is also very beneficial, and can be done to music to make it more interesting.

Remember, a tired gymnast is liable to take short cuts in execution, acquiring bad performance habits and increasing the chances of injury. Work on endurance often, slowly increasing the length of time spent at it.

Muscular endurance—work stunts in series or routines instead of one at a time, even if you have no intention of using these routines. Make the combinations short at first, increasing in length as your condition improves. *Do not neglect your strength work.* By increasing the number of repetitions of a strength exercise you are also increasing muscular endurance. Put an overload on your body by not giving in at the first sign of fatigue, but make sure that the stunts executed after that point are the ones which can be done with a minimum of conscious control—the ones which you have already well mastered.

In many cases, the two kinds of endurance cannot be separated. What benefits one will also benefit the other. Endurance is definitely needed for an effortless, enjoyable and well-finished performance.

Remember—only a well-tuned machine can give maximum performance. Do not be satisfied with less.

Outcomes

1. List the four areas that are most important in preparing one's body for gymnastics.
2. Where is flexibility most crucial?
3. Where is strength most needed?
4. What kind of endurance does a gymnast need?
5. Self-evaluation:
   a) In which of these areas do you need to improve most?
   b) List three exercises that could help you in these areas.
6. Why is stretching hip flexors important?
7. How do weight control and diet help a gymnast?

Concept VII—There Are Numerous Sources to Which the Aspiring Gymnast May Turn for Further Help in Increasing Her Skills

I. Organizations most prominent in the field of gymnastics:

a) Amateur Athletic Union, 231 West 58th St., New York, N.Y. 10019
b) American Sokol, 5611 Cermak Rd., Cicero, Ill.
c) American Turners, 1550 Clinton Ave. N., Rochester 21, N.Y.
d) United States Gymnastics Federation, P.O. Box 4699, Tucson, Ariz.

Write to any of these organizations, asking for the nearest active chapter or the representative in your area.

Other organizations dealing with gymnastics as a part of their program are:

a) National YMCA, 291 Broadway, New York, N.Y. 10007
b) Division of Girls' and Women's Sports of the American Association for Health, Physical Education and Recreation, 1201 16th St. N.W., Washington, D.C. 20036

Physical education teachers in local high schools or colleges are usually good sources of help in locating active gymnastics programs and resource people. They usually are among the first to be notified of any clinics or workshops in their vicinity, as well as active gymnastics camps during the summer.

II. Selected bibliography of books, periodicals and records:

General Books

Allison, June. *Advanced Gymnastics for Women.* New Rochelle, N.Y.: Sportshelf.

Babbitt, Diane and Haas, Werner. *Gymnastic Apparatus Exercises for Girls.* New York: The Ronald Press Company, 1964.

Cooper, Phyllis. *Feminine Gymnastics*. Minneapolis: Burgess Publishing Co.

Drury, Blanche and Schmid, Andrea. *Gymnastics for Women*. Palo Alto, Calif.: The National Press. (Record, Hoctor HLP-4011.)

Farkas, Jim. *Age-Group Gymnastics Workbook*. Tucson: The United States Gymnastics Federation Press.

Frederick, A. Bruce. *Women's Gymnastics*. Dubuque, Iowa: William C. Brown Company, Publishers, 1966.

Hughes, Eric. *Gymnastics for Girls*. New York: The Ronald Press Company, 1963.

Takemoto, M. and Hamada, S. *Women's Gymnastics*. Los Angeles: Frank Endo.

Yeager, Patrick. *A Teacher's Guide For Women's Gymnastics*. Statesboro, Ga.: Wide World Publications.

Specific Events
Periodicals, Records, Books

Drury, Blanche and Schmid, Andrea. "Free Exercise," Manual and Record. Hoctor Record HLP-4011, Waldwick, N.J.

Kjeldsen, Kitty. "Music for Intermediate and Advanced Floor Exercise." Hoctor Record HLP-4067.

Lienert, Walter J. *The Modern Girl Gymnast on the Uneven Parallel Bars*, 1010 West 64th St., Indianapolis, Ind.

Mademoiselle Gymnast. P.O. Box 777, Santa Monica, Calif. 90401

The Modern Gymnast. P.O. Box 611, Santa Monica, Calif. 90401

Prchal, Mildred. *Artistic Gymnastics, Floor Exercises*, Manual and Record. Hoctor Record HLP-4006.

Sjursen, Helen. *Balance Beam for Physical Educators and Competitors*. Hoctor Records, Waldwick, N.J.

————. "Floor Exercises for Girls and Women," Manual and Record. Dance Records, Inc., Waldwick, N.J.

————. *Uneven Bars for Physical Educators and Competitors*. Hoctor Records, Waldwick, N.J.

Yeager, Patrick. *Tumbling and Pyramids*. Wide World Publications, Statesboro, Ga.

Zuber, Dick. "Competitive Free Exercise." Hoctor Record HLP-3090.